Data Science

Textbook As Per CBSE Syllabus

Class 8th

Chandrika Jaini Vedam

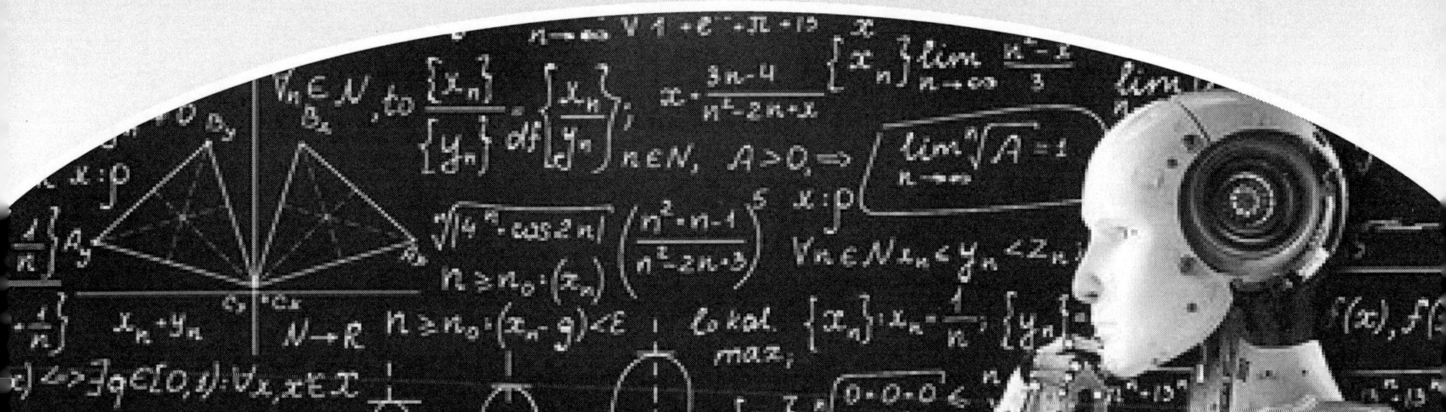

FIRST EDITION 2022

ISBN: 978-93-55510-53-2

Distributors:

BPB PUBLICATIONS
20, Ansari Road, Darya Ganj
New Delhi-110002
Ph: 23254990/23254991

DECCAN AGENCIES
4-3-329, Bank Street,
Hyderabad-500195
Ph: 24756967/24756400

MICRO MEDIA
Shop No. 5, Mahendra Chambers,
150 DN Rd. Next to Capital Cinema,
V.T. (C.S.T.) Station, MUMBAI-400 001
Ph: 22078296/22078297

BPB BOOK CENTRE
376 Old Lajpat Rai Market,
Delhi-110006
Ph: 23861747

Published by Manish Jain for BPB Publications, 20 Ansari Road, Darya Ganj, New Delhi-110002 and Printed at Manipal Technologies Limited, Manipal

About the Author

Chandrika Jaini Vedam is a writerpreneur and an ex-lecturer with more than two decades of involvement in the education industry. She has extensive experience in designing curricula and authoring books. She currently leads teams to develop content for educational AR/VR experiences, school textbooks and general books for children. She is an avid reader and an enthusiast of emerging technologies. Strong ethics and keeping creative abilities flowing are her mantra for developing good content. Globetrotting and gardening are her hobbies when she wants to break free from work. She is based out of the silicon-garden city of Bengaluru.

LinkedIn Profile: https://www.linkedin.com/in/chandrikavedam/

Preface

Data is omnipresent. It is everywhere. To collect and analyse data responsibly is the need of the hour. As Carly Fiorina, former executive, president, and chair of Hewlett-Packard says- "The goal is to turn data into information, and information into insight." Data Science is a vast field that should be taught at the school level, along with other subjects.

The book titled "Data Science" for class 8 covers the prescribed syllabus brought out by CBSE. This book aims to develop a readiness for understanding and appreciating Data Science and its applications in our lives. It introduces young learners to the world of data and explains the science behind it in an age-appropriate manner. The book encourages the student to think and learn constructively through interactive participation and engaging hands-on activities. Apart from introducing data science, the book also covers the relationship between data science and artificial intelligence.

It is our endeavour that the student learns the fundamentals in a crisp and clear graded manner. Though the book was developed with utmost care, any pointer towards an error will be duly noted and corrected.

Downloading the coloured images:

Please follow the link to download
the *Coloured Images* of the book:

https://rebrand.ly/254504

Errata

We take immense pride in our work at BPB Publications and follow best practices to ensure the accuracy of our content to provide with an indulging reading experience to our subscribers. Our readers are our mirrors, and we use their inputs to reflect and improve upon human errors if any, occurred during the publishing processes involved. To let us maintain the quality and help us reach out to any readers who might be having difficulties due to any unforeseen errors, please write to us at:

errata@bpbonline.com

Your support, suggestions and feedbacks are highly appreciated by the BPB Publications' Family.

BPB is searching for authors like you

If you're interested in becoming an author for BPB, please visit **www.bpbonline.com** and apply today. We have worked with thousands of developers and tech professionals, just like you, to help them share their insight with the global tech community. You can make a general application, apply for a specific hot topic that we are recruiting an author for, or submit your own idea.

The code bundle for the book is also hosted on GitHub at **https://github.com/bpbpublications/Data-Science-Textbook-For-Class-8th-As-per-CBSE-syllabus-**. In case there's an update to the code, it will be updated on the existing GitHub repository.

We also have other code bundles from our rich catalog of books and videos available at **https://github.com/bpbpublications**. Check them out!

PIRACY

If you come across any illegal copies of our works in any form on the internet, we would be grateful if you would provide us with the location address or website name. Please contact us at **business@bpbonline.com** with a link to the material.

If you are interested in becoming an author

If there is a topic that you have expertise in, and you are interested in either writing or contributing to a book, please visit **www.bpbonline.com**.

REVIEWS

Please leave a review. Once you have read and used this book, why not leave a review on the site that you purchased it from? Potential readers can then see and use your unbiased opinion to make purchase decisions, we at BPB can understand what you think about our products, and our authors can see your feedback on their book. Thank you!

For more information about BPB, please visit **www.bpbonline.com**.

Table of Contents

1 Introduction to Data

Objectives

After studying this chapter, you should be able to understand:

- Data and data source
- Quantitative and qualitative data
  - Discrete and continuous data
- Structured and unstructured data
- Real-world applications of data
  - Spam filtering
  - Biometrics
  - Web entertainment

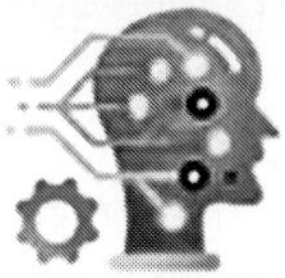

DATA AND DATA SOURCE

Data is the buzzword these days. It is everywhere- from your wardrobe to space stations. Data is limitless. Let us define it.

Figure 1.1: Data is limitless

Data, in simplest terms, is the collection of information. This information is collected from the environment around us. Humans use their five sense organs to collect data- they record what they see, hear, smell, feel and taste. In addition, they also record what they understand. Therefore, data is absorbed, stored, shared and transmitted.

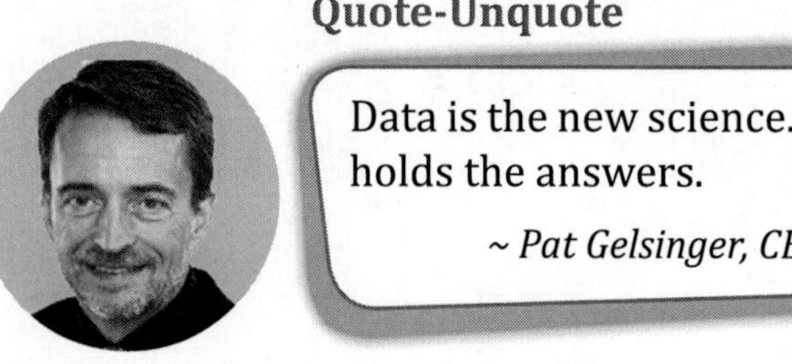

Quote-Unquote

Data is the new science. Big data holds the answers.

~ Pat Gelsinger, CEO of Intel

Data is collected from various sources. Anything and everything can be a **data source**. For example- a tea-seller can be a data source for the types of teas, the variety of tea recipes and even the types of customers. A lake can be a data source for aquatic plants and birds. A report card is a data source for performance in the class.

Figure 1.2: Tea seller is a data source for types of teas and customers

Figure 1.3: Lake with birds is a data source for aquatic life

Different data sources provide different types of data. However, a single data source can provide various types of data, or inversely, multiple data sources can provide the same kind of data. For example, a park is a data source for plants, people, types of swings etc. On the other hand, the same kind of data can be recorded from a school or a resort.

Figure 1.4: A park is a data source for plants, people, types of swings

Figure 1.5: School classroom is a data source for students, furniture, blackboard

Types of Data

Data is divided into various types when recorded on a computer. Broadly, these types are:

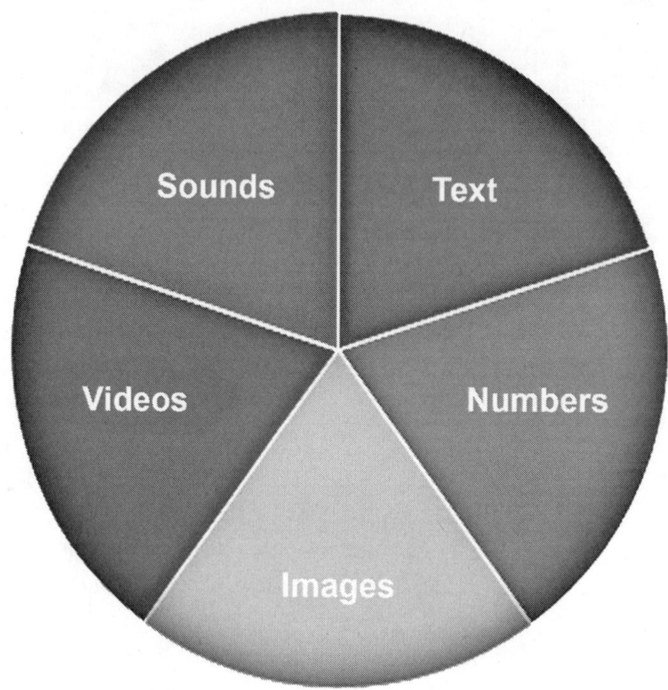

Figure 1.6: Types of data

QUANTITATIVE AND QUALITATIVE DATA

Data can be categorized, keeping in mind various factors. To begin with, we can divide data into:

- Quantitative data
- Qualitative data

While the **quantitative data** is factual and can be measured or counted, **qualitative** data is descriptive and cannot be counted.

Quantitative data is gathered by counting as opposed to qualitative data, which is gathered through observations.

Quantitative data is numeric in nature, and therefore, is analysed through statistics. Qualitative data, on the other hand, is analysed through categories.

Examples of quantitative data include marks, age, weight, number of patients, number of customers, etc. Colours of the flowers, contents of an email, hobbies, co-curricular activities are all examples of qualitative data.

Types of Quantitative Data

Quantitative data is further classified into:

- Discrete
- Continuous

While both discrete and continuous data are quantitative data types, they are numeric in nature. However, they are different. Whereas **discrete** data is both measurable and countable, **continuous** data is only measurable. Discrete data has clear spaces. Continuous data can have any intervals. Let us understand with some examples.

Figure 1.7: Continuous data

Consider a situation when we order a certain number of dishes in a restaurant. The number of dishes that we order is an example of discrete data, whereas the billed amount we pay is continuous data.

The number of students in a class is discrete data. Their body temperatures is an example of continuous data.

Figure 1.8: Discrete data

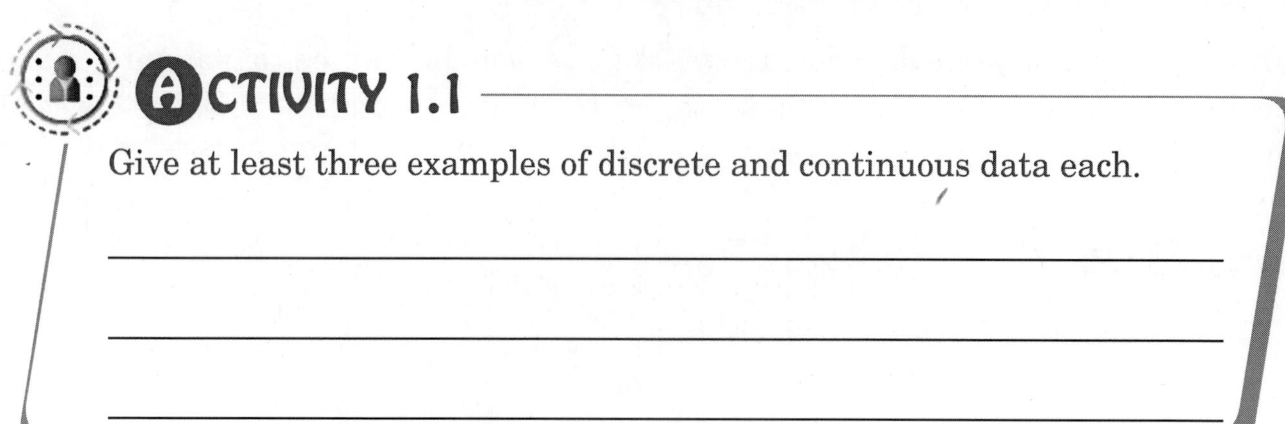

ACTIVITY 1.1

Give at least three examples of discrete and continuous data each.

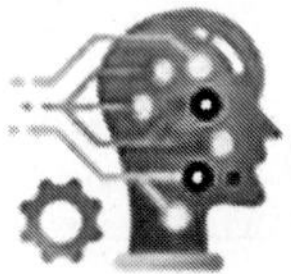

STRUCTURED AND UNSTRUCTURED DATA

Data may be **organised** (structured) or **unorganised** (unstructured).

Unstructured data should be organised; only then it can be analysed.

Look at the two images below. While the first one shows unstructured data, the second one displays structured data for the data in it is categorized and labelled.

Figure 1.9: Unstructured data

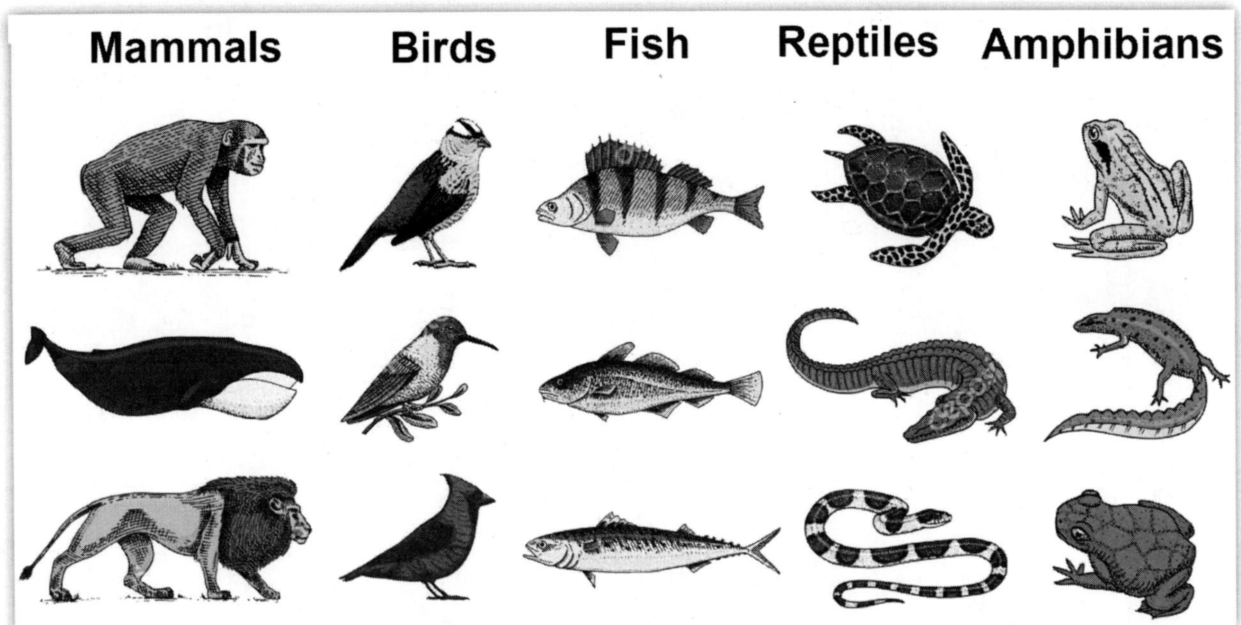

Figure 1.10: Structured data

Once the data is collected and organised, we try to **analyse** it.

Let us understand with an example. Look at the data shown in the figure 1.11. Is it understandable? Are you able to get some information out of it? No, because it is unorganised or unstructured. All we know is that there are some names and some numbers.

To organise data, it is placed into a table. This is called the **database table**. In other words, a database table contains organised data. Data in a database table is organised in **rows** and **columns**.

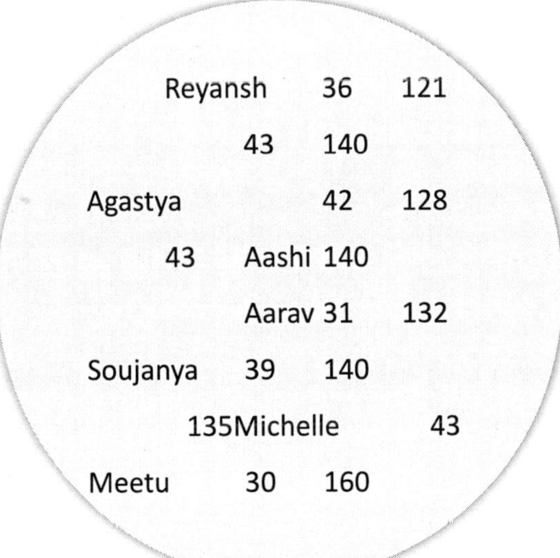

Figure 1.11: Unorganized data

Let us now arrange the data (shown earlier) into a table. Further investigation states that the data covers the names of people and their respective weights and heights. An organised data in a table is thus generated, as shown below.

Name	Weight	Height
Reyansh	36	121
Agastya	42	128
Aashi	43	140
Aarav	31	132
Soujanya	39	135
Michelle	29	125
Meetu	30	160

Table 1.1: Organised data in a table

Each column in the table represents a variable. A variable is an entity that contains some value. In the above example, all columns (Name, Weight and Height) represent variables and each variable has seven observations, arranged in rows as records.

Create a table which records the daily morning, afternoon and night temperatures for a week- from Monday to Sunday.

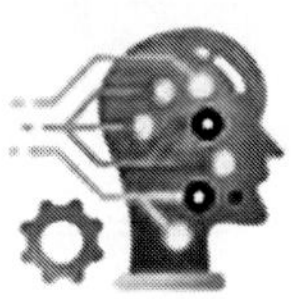

REAL-WORLD APPLICATIONS OF DATA

Data is used everywhere these days. No organisation or entity can survive without managing data. Though there are thousands of applications of data, we have a listed a few for you.

Spam Filtering

By now, most of you would have your own email ids. Have you ever wondered how some emails automatically go to the inbox while others end up in the spam folder? This is accomplished through data science. **Spam filters** (machine programs) are taught to recognise certain words in the mail, which classify them as spam. The program is trained using thousands of emails. After it gets trained, it segregates spam mails easily.

Figure 1.12: Spam filtering

Biometrics

Biometrics refers to the physical features of a human being, which are unique in every person. These include finger and thumbprints, DNA, eye iris, etc.

An individual's biometric information is recorded database. Various agencies like police, offices, bank lockers, etc., use biometrics software to detect the presence of employees, customers, criminals, etc. even schools use biometrics these days to mark the entry or exit of students, teachers and other staff members.

Figure 1.13: Biometrics

Web Entertainment

Many people watch content over different platforms on the Internet. Some examples of entertainment platforms are YouTube, Facebook videos, IMDB, Netflix and many more.

Have you ever wondered how these platforms suggest a listing for you every time you log in? How do they come to know about your likes without asking you? This is because of **data**

Figure 1.14: Web entertainment

analysis. The backend programs, over a period of time, monitor which types of videos you play frequently. These programs get trained by this data and start predicting your choices. Hence the suggestions.

Figure 1.15: Reco engine

Ecommerce websites follow the same process. They monitor your purchases and suggest choices accordingly.

Such programs are given a special name- **Reco Engines**.

Remember, data is powerful; data is the future.

POINTS TO REMEMBER

- Data is limitless.
- Data is collected from the environment around us.
- Data is collected from various sources.
- Data is divided into various types when recorded on a computer.
- Data can be categorised, keeping in mind various factors.
- Data may be organised (structured) or unorganised (unstructured).
- Once the data is collected and organised, we try to analyse it.
- Data in a database table is organised in rows and columns.

GLOSSARY

- **Data:** It is the collection of information.
- **Data source:** It is the source from where data is collected.
- **Quantitative data:** It is factual and can be measured or counted.
- **Qualitative data:** It is descriptive and cannot be counted.
- **Discrete data:** It is both measurable and countable.
- **Continuous data:** It is only measurable.
- **Unstructured data:** It is unorganised data.
- **Structured data:** It is organised data.
- **Database table:** It contains organised data in rows and columns.
- **Variable:** Itis an entity that contains some value.

EXERCISE

Multiple choice questions.

1. Data is collected from various sources.

   a. True ☐ b. False ☐

2. Data can be:

   a. Absorbed and stored ☐ b. Shared and transmitted ☐

   c. Organised and analysed ☐ d. All of the above ☐

3. Unorganised data can be stored in a table.

   a. True ☐ b. False ☐

4. While the quantitative data is factual and can be measured or counted, qualitative data is descriptive and cannot be counted.

   a. True ☐ b. False ☐

5. Each column in a data table represents a -

a. Constant ☐ b. Variable ☐

6. What is organised data called?

a. Structured ☐ b. Unstructured ☐

c. Special ☐ d. Sensitive ☐

7. Number of months in a year is an example of-

a. Discrete Data ☐ b. Continuous Data ☐

8. A database table consists of-

a. Loops and iterations ☐ b. Shapes and smart art ☐

c. Unorganised data ☐ d. Rows and columns ☐

9. Discrete and continuous data is numeric in nature.

a. True ☐ b. False ☐

10. A variable is an entity that contains no value.

a. True ☐ b. False ☐

11. Which of the following data do we get from a park?

a. Plants ☐ b. Books ☐

c. Cars ☐ d. Grocery ☐

12. What are spam filters taught to recognise?

a. Certain words ☐ b. Images ☐

c. Punctuation ☐ d. Nouns ☐

13. Biometrics refers to which of the following?

a. Height ☐ b. Weight ☐

c. Fingerprints ☐ d. Nationality ☐

14. YouTube, Netflix, Facebook Videos are examples of which of the following industry?

a. Web Design ☐ b. WordPress ☐

c. Entertainment ☐ d. Health and fitness ☐

15. Which programs monitor your purchases and offer suggestions?

a. Blogging ☐ b. Spam Filters ☐

c. Search Engines ☐ d. Reco Engines ☐

Answer the following questions in short (100 words).

1. Define data and mention its types.

____

____

____

____

2. Differentiate between structured and unstructured data.

____

____

____

____

3. What is a data source? Explain with an example.

____

____

____

____

4. What is the prerequisite for analysing data?

____

____

5. What is discrete and continuous data?

6. What kind of data can a single data source provide?

7. What kind of data is required when we order dishes in a restaurant and the amount of bill we pay?

8. Mention the steps involved after collection of data to its analysis.

9. What is spam filtering?

10. Explain biometrics.

11. What is web entertainment?

12. What programs do e-commerce websites use to monitor preferences?

Answer in detail (150 words).

1. Write a note on different categories of data.

2. Explain discrete and continuous data.

3. Explain how entertainment platforms make use of data analysis.

4. How is data organised in a database table? Explain with an example.

5. Explain how spam is filtered using data science.

HOTS

Higher Order Thinking Skills

1. You have visited a movie theatre. Make a list of five types of discrete data that you can collect from there.

2. List five types of continuous data that you can collect from a clinic.

Applied Project

Discuss how data analytics is applied in following features.

- Autocorrect, and
- Autocomplete

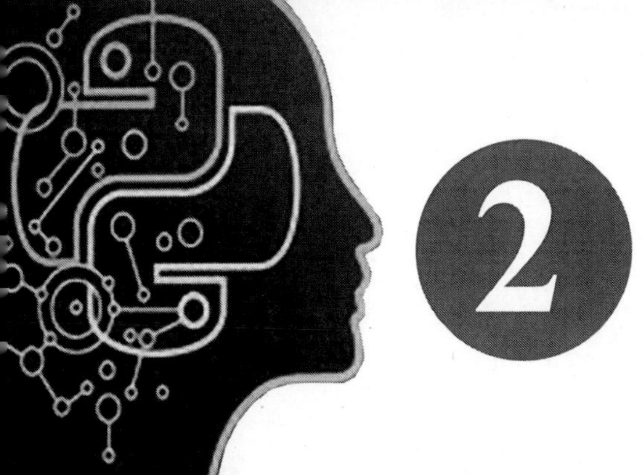

2 Introduction to Data Science

Objectives

After studying this chapter, you should be able to understand:

- What data science is?
- Why is data important?
- Applications of data science
- Careers in data science
- What does data science help us achieve?

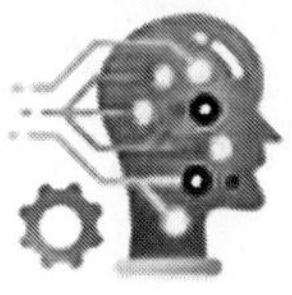

INTRODUCTION TO DATA SCIENCE

Artificial Intelligence is an umbrella term for a broad range of domains. It is a known fact now that Artificial Intelligence will play a significant role in our future. Leading technologies behind Artificial Intelligence are explained below. Data Science is one of them, which we will study in detail in this chapter.

1. **Data science (Data collection and analyses)** is like nutrition to AI. The aim of the data science is to structure data, making it interpretable and easy to work with. It feeds on data and learns from it. Related data is collected from multiple sources in many ways, and then it gets interpreted and analysed based on its meaningfulness to the business problem at hand.
2. **Computer vision** is an area of AI concerned with how computers see and understand digital images and videos.

Quote-Unquote

Data is a precious thing and will last longer than the systems themselves.

~ Tim Berners-Lee
Inventor of the World Wide Web

3. **Machine learning (algorithm)** is concerned with the design and development of algorithms that allow computers to evolve behaviours based on experimental data.
4. **Natural language processing** is an area of AI concerned with the interactions between a computer and human languages.
5. **Expert system** is a computer system that emulates, or acts in all respects, with the decision-making capabilities of a human expert.
6. **Automated speech recognition** is similar to natural language processing and is concerned with the meaning of sounds.

WHY IS DATA SO IMPORTANT?

If anything is ruling this world today, then it is **electricity**. In fact, many people compare **data** to modern-day electricity. Experts believe that we will not be able to perceive our lives without data after a few years. It will be as crucial as electricity these days.

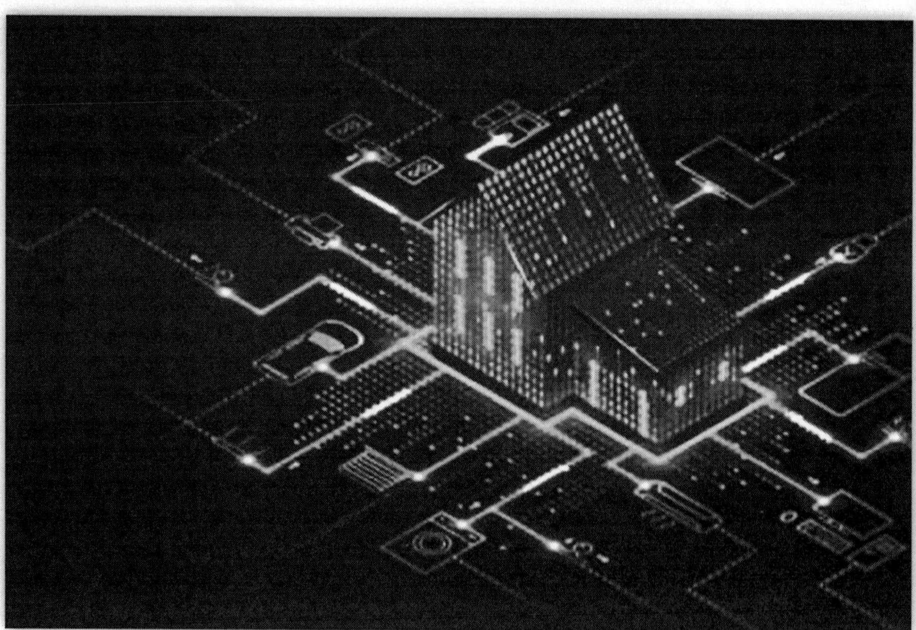

Figure 2.1: Data is everywhere

Data is everywhere, and new technologies are emerging that utilise data to bring out smart products. In simplest terms, the science of studying data is called **data science**.

ACTIVITY 2.1

Visit the following URL to play the Rock, Paper Scissors game against an AI model at least 10 times. Observe how it uses the data collected from your moves to play against you.

https://www.afiniti.com/corporate/rock-paper-scissors

Now, answer the following questions.

- How many times did the AI model win?

  ____

- How many times did you win?

  ____

- Did you apply any strategy?

  ____

WHAT IS DATA SCIENCE?

Data Science is a field that involves a combined study of scientific methods, mathematics, statistics and coding to develop a system. Such a system extracts meaningful insights from data.

Data Science helps to create intelligent systems. Such systems are capable of taking independent decisions. They are based on old and new datasets (collection of the same type or related data) available.

Data scientists develop machine learning algorithms (programs) using their knowledge in the domains mentioned earlier to produce AI systems, which bring out hidden information when applied to data. They use a wide range of tools, such as Python, R,

Tableau, GitHub, Apache Spark, Hadoop and SQL and many more to accomplish this.

Data professionals are much in demand these days as they draw meaningful insights from data to assist companies in making profitable business decisions. For example, companies like Amazon, Prime Video, Facebook, LinkedIn use recommendation systems for their members. A **recommendation engine** is a set of algorithms that keeps track of the user behaviour on a website and based on that, makes suggestions for products/ entities/ people that the user might be interested in.

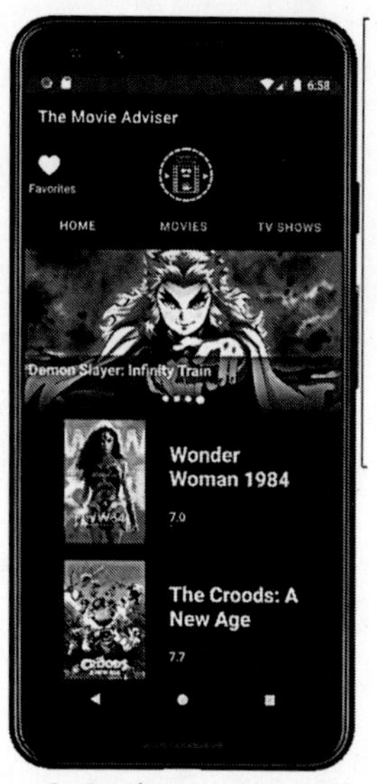

Figure 2.2: A reco engine in a mobile app

APPLICATIONS OF DATA SCIENCE

Though the scope of applications of data sciences is broad, we have divided them into the following categories:

Fraud Detection

More and more banks are making use of intelligent systems to track transactions made by credit cards holders. This helps them in detecting fraudulent activities, thereby labelling the customers or transactions as fraudulent or genuine. Banks use smart systems for insurance and accounting also. They analyse the investment patterns of customers and suggest offers and more investments. An unexpected change in data patterns can often be a sign of something going wrong or possible fraud.

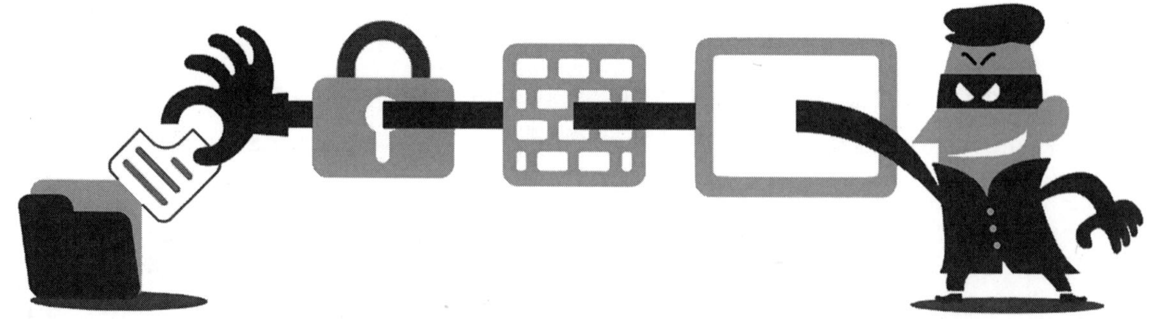

Figure 2.3: Intelligent systems catch fraud transactions

Healthcare

There is a huge impact of data science on healthcare. The various industries in healthcare that use data science are:

- Genetics and Genomics
- Predictive Modelling for Diagnosis

Genetics and Genomics: Data Science helps find biological connections between genetics, risk of diseases, and drug response. An intelligent model applies statistical techniques to genomic sequences, allowing scientists to understand the complexities of genetic structures in detail.

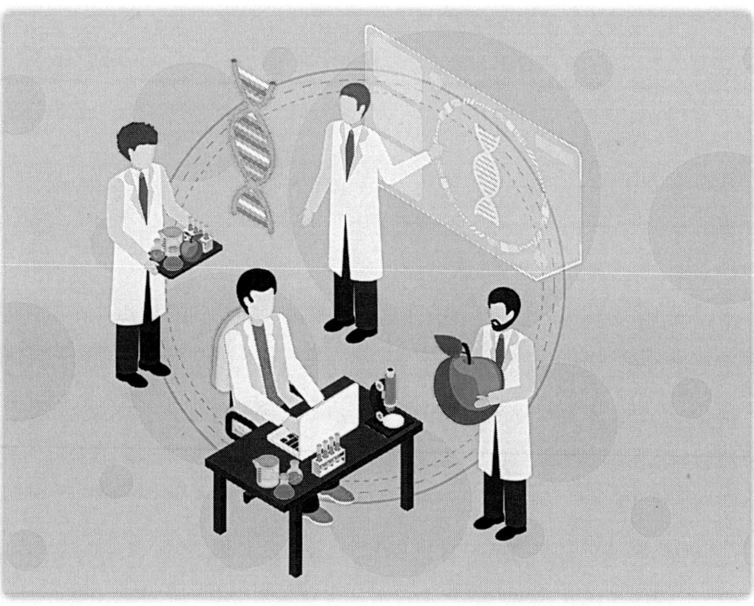

Figure 2.4: Data science in healthcare sector

Genetic risk prediction is a giant leap towards more personalised healthcare. **Predictive modelling** helps to predict the outcome of a diagnosis given the previous data of the patients. Therefore, it provides helpful insights to doctors and medical practitioners.

Imagine a system predicting how well a person will respond to medicine by simply collecting and analysing data based on his past health.

Internet Searches

Data Science is evolving Internet searches. All the search engines, such as Google, Bing, AOL, etc., use data science algorithms to bring out results for the searched query. All this is done in a fraction of seconds!

Figure 2.5: Data science has evolved Internet

E-commerce

One of the primary industries to benefit from data sciences is retail and e-commerce. It is used not just for forecasting sales of goods and services but also for predicting trends. In addition, these intelligent systems identify a potential customer base while optimising price structures for a particular section of consumers.

Data Science is also applied to the feedback provided by the customers. This is called **sentiment analysis**.

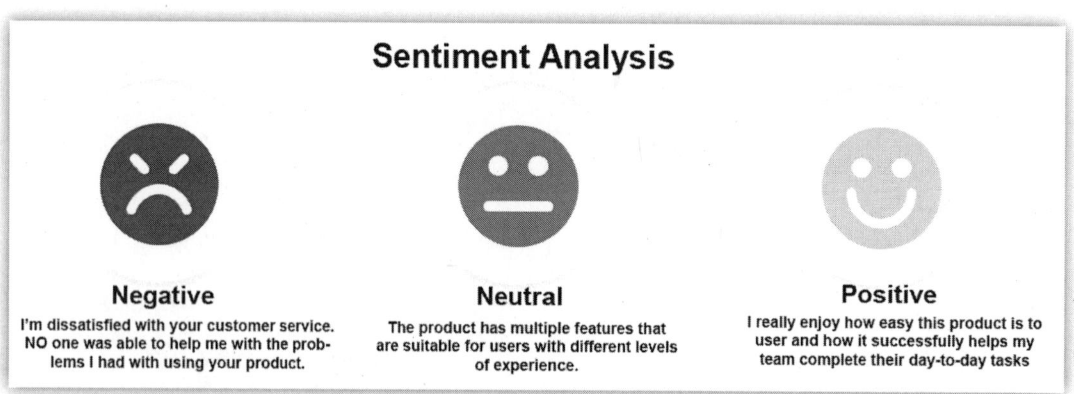

Figure 2.6: Sentiment analysis

Furthermore, fraud detection through data sciences is used for finding fraud customers and merchants.

The **targeted advertising** is another segment of e-commerce that focuses on the digital marketing spectrum. Data science algorithms track user's past searches and surfing on the Internet to display ad banners on various websites.

Figure 2.7: Targeted advertising through data science

Manufacturing

Data Science helps manufacturing industries to develop autonomous systems that help promote production to new levels. Smart systems for industries have enabled companies to predict problems and find solutions. Data Science also helps industries monitor product quality, costs, hours, and other such variables.

Transport

Data Science has been most impactful in developing intelligent vehicles, such as **self-driving** cars. These are also known as **driverless cars**.

Data Science has also helped make smart systems that monitor routes and share details with the drivers in real-time. For example, if a route is congested, the system suggests an alternate route. They also monitor fuel consumption patterns, vehicle routes, breakdowns, etc. Intelligent models continuously inspect driving environments for drivers. The goal is to provide safe environments.

Figure 2.8: Route monitoring with the help of data science

ACTIVITY 2.2

Find out and write the names of five companies that are manufacturing driverless cars.

____

____

Apart from road transport, data science has also impacted air transport. Various airlines use smart systems to predict flight arrivals and delays, project the most lucrative routes between two destinations, and monitor customer behaviour regarding booking dates, seats, destinations, etc.

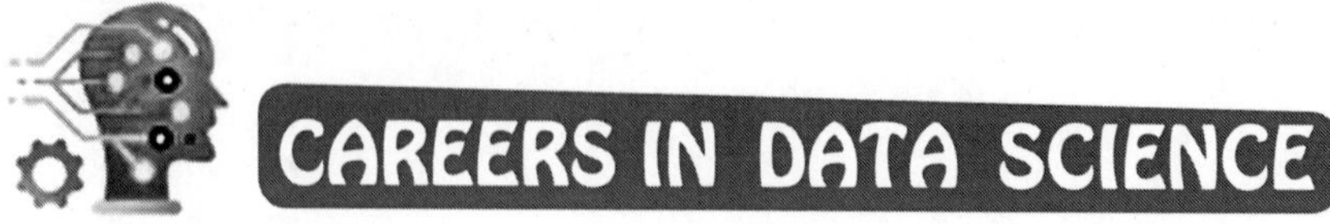

CAREERS IN DATA SCIENCE

We all know that data science needs the skills shown below. Many people are gaining these skills to jump into the broader field of AI and its subset data science.

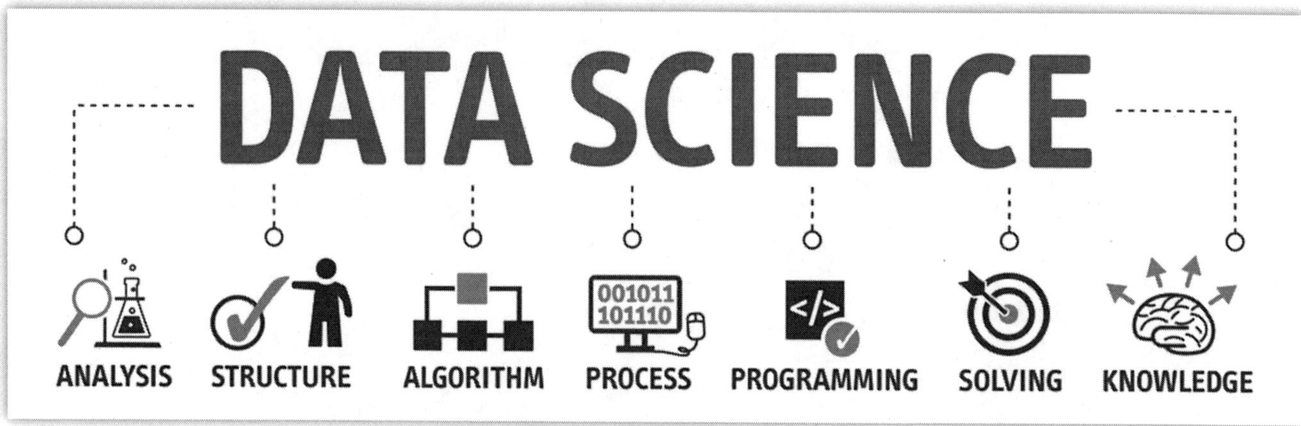

Figure 2.9: Skills needed for data science

Careers in the field of data science are mushrooming at a large scale. Various job profiles related to data science are developed to cater to the needs of the organisations. Companies like Google, Microsoft, Amazon and many more are expanding manifold in the field of applied data science. Some of these job titles are explained below.

Data Scientists look for problem areas, examine the current trends and predict the future ones. Knowledge in mathematics, statistics, and computer science helps data scientists develop actionable plans for organisations after studying a huge amount of data, structured or unstructured (big data).

Data Analysts analyse the data and examine the trends. They work on specific problems and analyse structured data. Their knowledge in mathematics, statistics and computer science helps them create AI models.

Many times, the roles of Data Scientists and Data Analysts are thought to be the same. This is not true. However, together they work upon structured and unstructured data to predict future trends.

Data Engineers/ Architects are the creators of the database in an organisation. Their job is to oversee data handling at all levels, including classification. We can say that they are the managers of large amounts of data in an organisation. They work with other data professionals to build a robust database that gives meaningful and insightful information. They are mainly software engineers with high-level coding capabilities.

Business Analysts/ Business Intelligence Analysts are the subsets of data analysts. However, they are more focused on the impact of data on the business or the market. They tell their organisation which project to follow and how to strategise. Knowledge in business administration is a plus, along with math, statistics and computer science, for business analysts.

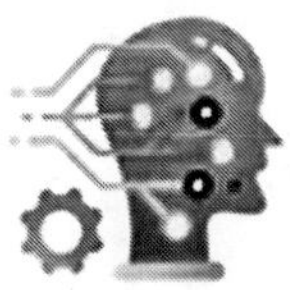

WHAT DOES DATA SCIENCE HELP US ACHIEVE?

Data Science helps us to collect data that could be of use to an organisation. It helps the organisation to target its objectives with a meaningful approach to achieve the goals. The data scientist gets the data collected and analysed. This data is available either online or even offline. Online data collection sources include:

- Digital records of the organisation
- Government Portals
- Reliable Websites, such as Kaggle
- World Organisations' open-sourced statistical websites

Offline sources of data are surveys, observations and interviews.

ACTIVITY 2.3

Visit the following URL: https://www.india.gov.in/topics/environment-forest

1. Click on the Open Data tab.
2. Click on any of the links and try and download a file.

- Were you successful?

  ____

- In which format did you download a file?

  ____

When a large amount of data is collected, there may be some errors too. Let us look at some instances.

1. **Inaccurate data:** Inaccurate data value is an incorrect value in a dataset. For example, a name entered in a marks field. Another possibility of inaccurate data is when the value entered becomes invalid. Such a value is displayed as the NaN value in the dataset. This becomes a null value, and hence, meaningless. Such values are removed from the database.
2. **Missing data:** Such data values are not erroneous values. These are simply missing from the dataset, and therefore, the cell remains empty.
3. **Outliers:** An outlier is a data point in a dataset that doesn't fall in the range of other observations. They are plotted distinct from the other values and are termed as outliers as they do not belong to the range of data.

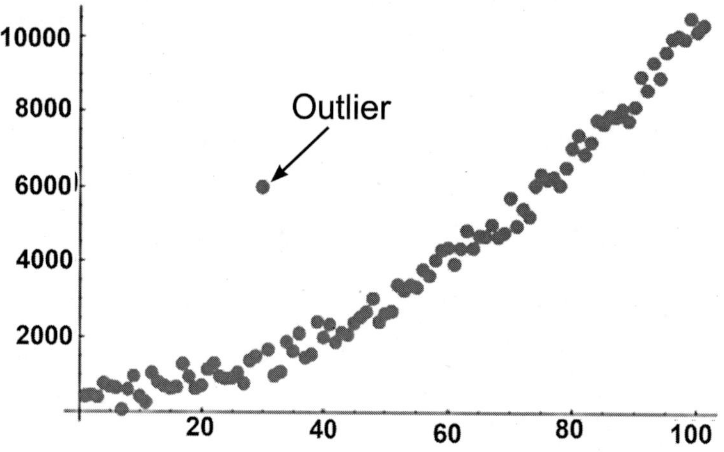

Figure 2.10: An outlier spotted in a chart

Once the data is collected, it needs to be visualised in order to understand patterns.

Next is the data modelling stage, which actually integrates intelligence in the machine and develops a solution model based on the analyses of collected and filtered data. During the data modelling,

- Different variables are studied and relationships are explored between them.
- **Exploratory Data Analytics (EDA)**, which comprises statistical formulae and visualisation tools, is made use of.
- Training and testing data is produced.

- Analysis techniques like **classification** and **clustering** determine whether the current model will be viable or not.

Techniques to analyse data widely depend on its type. The model looks for patterns and relationships between the existing data, called the testing data, and the required prediction in data science.

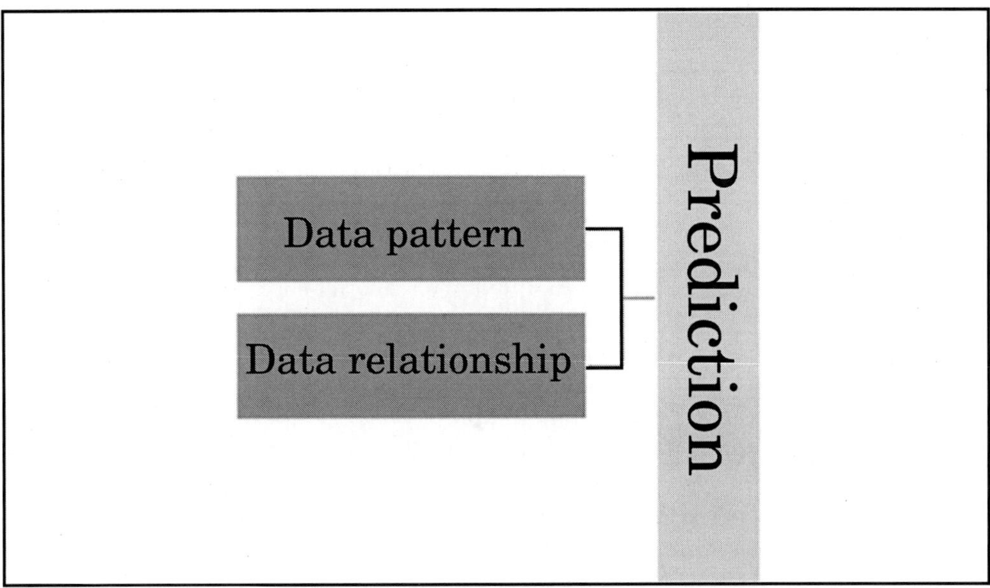

Figure 2.11: Making predictions

Then, new data is introduced to the model. This is called **training data**. The model's accuracy gets better and better when exposed to more and more training data. In order to achieve this, appropriate techniques, such as supervised and unsupervised, are followed.

The **supervised technique** is also known as the **classification** technique. This method classifies data with the help of class labels. An example of classification technique is as follows:

A customer is considered as safe/ risky according to his Blood Pressure readings and Age in the health insurance application process. This is supervised learning, where the goal is to build a model which can classify new data. Training and testing datasets are used in model development.

In the above example, since the outcome will be one of the two choices (safe or risky), it is called **binary classification**. If there are more than two choices, we use a multiclass classification.

Application ID	Age	BP Reading	Safe/Risky
Cust_001	43	110/75	Safe
Cust_002	27	180/100	Risky
Cust_003	52	120/100	Risky
Cust_004	18	110/79	Safe
Cust_005	33	120/85	Safe
Cust_006	45	128/102	Risky
Cust_007	29	180/80	Risky
Cust_008	51	120/80	Safe
Cust_009	71	110/80	Risky
Custo_010	60	119/80	Safe

Table 2.1: Binary classification

On the other hand, the **unsupervised technique** is also known as the **clustering** technique. Though it is similar to classification, it doesn't give data any labels. An example of clustering is a grouping of students in a class according to their learning behaviour. Another example is clustering diagnostic treatments together as per their effect on patients.

Therefore, we can say that major differences between classification and clustering are as follows:

Classification	Clustering
Is used for supervised learning.	Is used for unsupervised learning.
Dataset is organised under labels.	Dataset is not organised under labels.
Training and testing data is used.	Training and testing data is not used.
Is more complex.	Is less complex.

Reinforcement learning is another technique of machine learning. It is feedback-based, meaning that the program learns to behave in an environment by performing the actions and getting feedback on the results of actions. A good result generates positive feedback, whereas a bad result generates negative feedback. This can be considered as 'reward' or 'punishment'. As more and more data is fed, the model/ machine is reinforced with positive behaviour. As a result, it learns to give correct outputs.

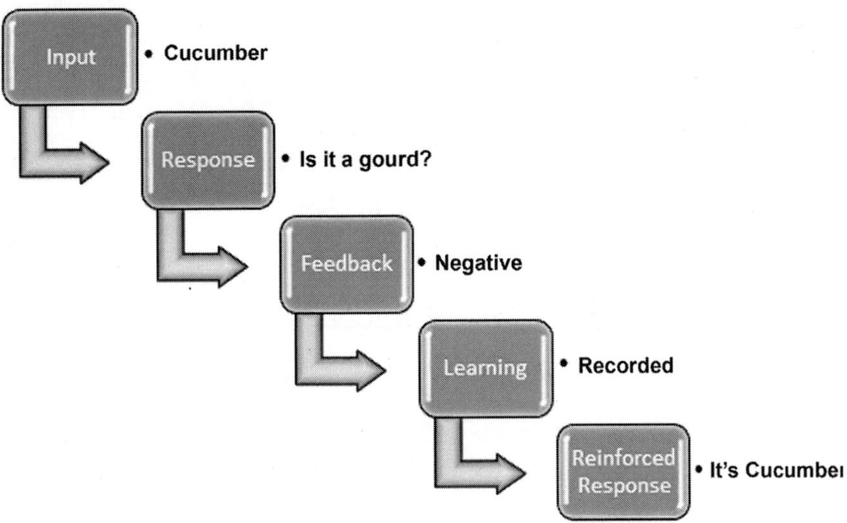

Figure 2.12: Reinforced learning

An upcoming application of reinforcement ML is in *industrial robotics*.

ACTIVITY 2.4

See how self-driving cars are taught to drive using reinforcement learning at the following link:

https://wayve.ai/blog/learning-to-drive-in-a-day-with-reinforcement-learning

Regression is a method mainly used for making predictions based on some numerical values (stored in variables). The output of regression is also numeric. This forecasting method is mostly used for predicting weather conditions, making sales targets, looking at future marketing trends, etc.

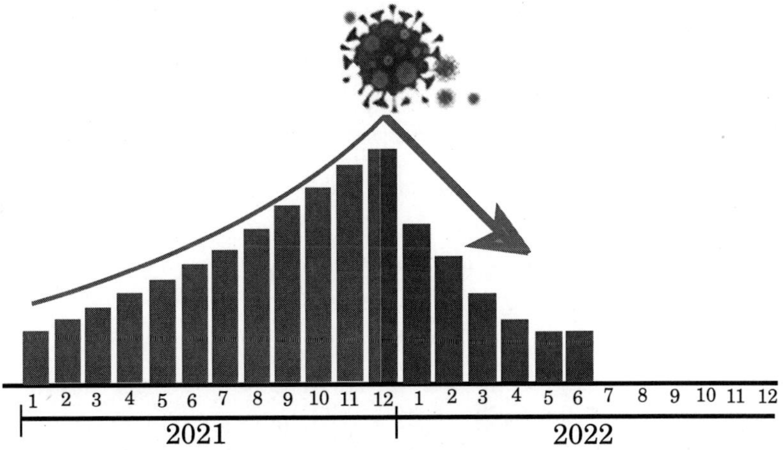

Figure 2.13: Regression

POINTS TO REMEMBER

- Artificial Intelligence is an umbrella term for a broad range of domains.
- The main technologies behind artificial intelligence are data science, computer vision, machine learning, natural language processing, expert system and automated speech recognition.
- Data is everywhere and new technologies are emerging that utilise data to bring out smart products.
- Data Science is a field that involves a combined study of scientific methods, mathematics, statistics and programming to develop a system that can extract meaningful insights from data.
- Though the scope of applications of data sciences is broad, we have divided them into – fraud detection, internet searches, healthcare, e-commerce, manufacturing and transport.
- When a large amount of data is collected, it is possible that there are some errors too. These could be inaccurate data, missing data and outliers.
- Data can be of various types, such as numerical, categorical and ordinal.
- In data science, a model looks for patterns and relationships between the data and the required prediction.
- That model tries to make predictions for new datasets which it has never seen before.

GLOSSARY

- **Data Science (Data collection and analyses):** It is the field that involves a combined study of scientific methods, mathematics, statistics and programming to develop a system that can extract meaningful insights from data.
- **Computer vision:** It is the area of AI concerned with how computers can see and understand digital images and videos.

- **Machine learning (algorithms):** It involves designing and developing algorithms that allow computers to evolve behaviours based on experimental data.
- **Natural language processing:** It is the area of AI concerned with the interactions between a computer and human languages.
- **Expert system:** It is the computer system that emulates, or acts in all respects, with the decision-making capabilities of a human expert.
- **Classification:** This method is used for supervised learning; dataset is organised under labels.
- **Clustering:** This method is used for unsupervised learning; dataset is not organised under labels.
- **Outlier:** It is the data point in a dataset that doesn't fall in the range of other observations.
- **Supervised technique:** It is also known as the classification technique; it classifies data with the help of class labels.
- **Unsupervised technique:** It is also known as the clustering technique; it doesn't give data any labels.
- **Reinforcement learning:** Another technique of machine learning; it is a feedback-based system, meaning that the program learns to behave in an environment by performing the actions and getting feedback on the results of actions.
- **Regression:** It is a method mainly used for making predictions based on some numerical values (stored in variables).

EXERCISE

Multiple choice questions.

1. What is the aim of data science?

a. Share data ☐ b. Interpret data ☐

c. Delete data ☐ d. Map data ☐

2. Natural Language Processing is an area of AI concerned with the interactions between a computer and human languages.

a. True ☐ b. False ☐

3. Which technology behind Artificial Intelligence has helped to create intelligent systems capable of making autonomous decisions based on old and new datasets?

a. Expert System ☐

b. Data Science ☐

c. Natural Language Processing ☐

d. Automated Speech Recognition ☐

4. More and more banks are using intelligent systems to track transactions made by credit cardholders. Which application of data science has been referred to here?

a. Fraud detection ☐ b. Healthcare ☐

c. E-commerce ☐ d. Manufacturing ☐

5. In which sector do data science help industries monitor product quality, costs, hours, and other such variables?

a. Transport ☐ b. Healthcare ☐

c. E-commerce ☐ d. Manufacturing ☐

6. Which of the following is not included in the offline sources of data?

a. Interviews ☐ b. Government portals ☐

c. Observations ☐ d. Survey ☐

7. When a large amount of data is collected, it is possible that there are some errors too. Which of the following is not an error?

a. Inadequacy ☐ b. Inaccurate data ☐

c. Missing data ☐ d. Outliers ☐

8. Grouping of students in a class according to their learning behaviour is an example of?

a. Clustering ☐ b. Classification ☐

c. Categorisation ☐ d. Modelling ☐

9. What is the name for a set of algorithms that keep track of the user behaviour on a website and based on that, make suggestions for products/entities/people that the user might be interested in?

   a. Machine learning algorithms ☐
   b. Reco engine ☐
   c. Computer Vision ☐
   d. Deep Learning ☐

10. Data scientists use which of the following tools?

   a. Facebook, Pinterest, Twitter ☐
   b. Word, excel and notepad ☐
   c. Photoshop, pictures, and videos ☐
   d. Python, R, Tableau, GitHub ☐

11. Banks secure their operations through which smart systems?

   a. Customer income and gifts ☐
   b. Track transactions and fraud detections ☐
   c. Loans and interest ☐
   d. Shares and dividends ☐

12. What do search engines Google, Bing, AOL, etc., use to bring out results for the searched query?

   a. Structured data search ☐
   b. Library search records ☐
   c. Social security information ☐
   d. Data science algorithms ☐

13. The field of data science is expanding and data scientists are in high demand. Data scientists can get jobs in which companies?

   a. Google ☐ b. Microsoft ☐
   c. Asian Paints ☐ d. Amazon ☐

14. While collecting a huge quantity of data, errors can occur. Which of the following is a data error?

a. Outliers ☐ b. Data table ☐

c. Numerical data ☐ d. Predictive analysis ☐

15. Data Science is a field that involves a combined study of which of the following to develop a system that can extract meaningful insights from data?

a. Entertainment, movies and music ☐

b. Transport, communication and trade ☐

c. e-commerce, banking and finance ☐

d. Scientific methods, mathematics, statistics, and programming ☐

16. Which forecasting method is mostly used for predicting weather conditions, making sales targets, looking at future marketing trends, etc.?

a. Progression ☐ b. Regression ☐

c. Digression ☐ d. Interpolation ☐

Answer the following questions in short (100 words).

1. Define data science.

____

____

____

____

2. What is an expert system?

____

____

____

3. Why is data so important?

4. Mention one way in which data science helps in e-commerce.

5. List any three career roles for data science.

6. How is a data scientist different from a data analyst?

7. Which technique of data science will you use when the segregation output is yes/no? Define it.

8. How does predictive modelling help?

9. What is sentiment analysis?

10. What is the role of data analysts?

11. Explain reinforcement learning.

12. What is a supervised technique?

13. Define clustering.

14. What does data science help us to achieve?

15. Define regression.

Answer in detail (150 words).

1. Mention any three applications of data science.

2. Differentiate between classification and clustering.

3. What is the impact of data science on the transport industry?

4. Differentiate between supervised and unsupervised techniques.

5. What is reinforced learning? Explain with an example diagram.

HOTS Higher Order Thinking Skills

You already know who data analysts are. Now find out about environmental data analysts. You can read about this sector at the following URL:

https://www.environmentalscience.org/career/environmental-data-analyst

After reading the article, list any five special skills needed to become an environmental data analyst.

____

____

____

____

____

____

____

____

Applied Project

You have been given the description of 100 dogs. Now, you have to group them as per their size and colour. Which technique would you use? Give example labels that you would use to group them, three for size and three for colour.

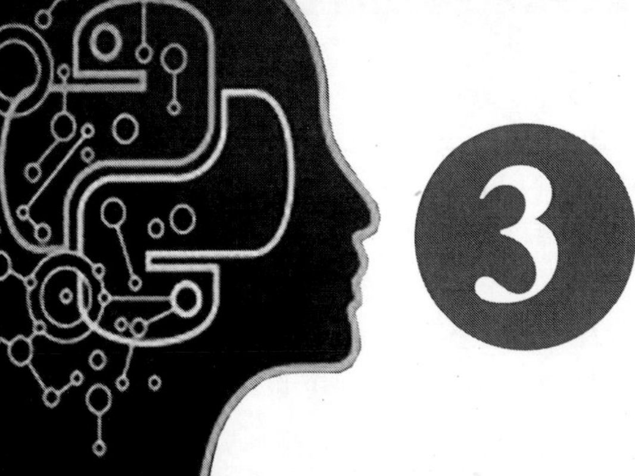

3 DATA VISUALISATION

Objectives

After studying this chapter, you should be able to understand:

- The life cycle of data
- Project definition
- Data collection
- Data visualisation
- Why is data visualisation important?
- Visualisation tools

LIFE CYCLE OF DATA

The life cycle of data science passes through various stages. We will learn about these in this chapter. However, please note that Data Modelling and Evaluation and Deployment are out of the scope of the syllabus.

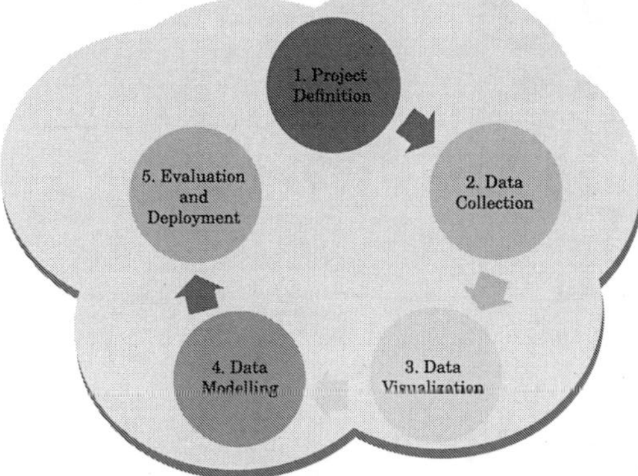

Figure 3.1: Life cycle of data science

PROJECT DEFINITION

This stage defines the project requirements. It outlines the business problem and budget. The initial suggestions and the plans to achieve the goals are formed at this stage.

DATA COLLECTION

This stage is when the data professionals collect the data. After the business problem is identified, data related to it is collected. This data is gathered from various sources. These are called **data sources**. These sources are available either online or even offline. Let us look at some of them.

Online data collection sources include:

Figure 3.2: Digital records of the organisation

Figure 3.3: Government portals

Figure 3.4: Reliable websites, such as Kaggle

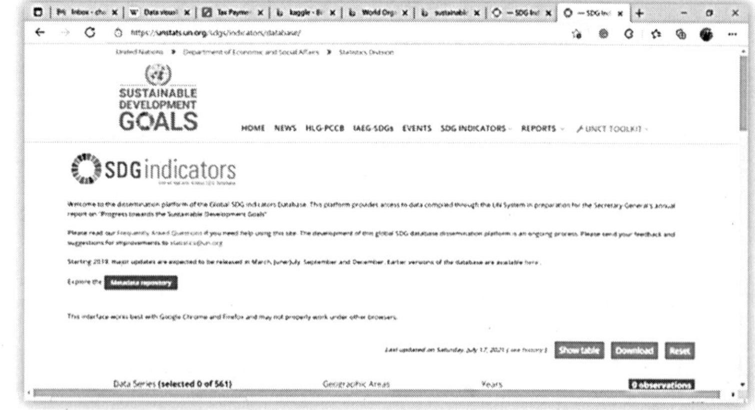

Figure 3.5: World Organisations' statistical websites

Offline sources of data are **surveys**, **observations** and **interviews**.

Figure 3.6. Offline sources

ACTIVITY 3.1

Imagine you are in a shopping mall. What all kinds of data can you collect from there?

____

____

Data scientists use software to gather and place data in a format which would later be analysed. Numeric and alphanumeric data is collected and stored in tables for later use.

Many organisations, such as banks, schools, hospitals, travel agencies, etc., have their records stored in databases. However, these are not available for everyone to access. Therefore, proper permissions should be taken while collecting data, or data available for public usage should be collected. One should never breach someone's privacy to collect data. Data should be acquired from reliable sources only.

Figure 3.7. Data stored in an Excel sheet

The collected data in tables is next stored in different formats, such as MS Excel, by the data scientists.

DATA VISUALISATION

Data visualisation means displaying data pictorially, either through graphs and charts. Data is visually represented to give clear information to the users. It is one of the steps in data analysis or data science. To convey ideas effectively, we must provide insights into complex data in a more interesting manner.

Figure 3.8: Data visualisation is essential

Most organisations use automated visualisation charting tools because these allow a quick and straightforward view of the most relevant features of a dataset. This step helps the analyst to identify the important variables in the dataset. By displaying data through various types of charts, for example, bar charts, scatter and density plots, etc., analysts can study the variables and relationships between them. This helps them decide if further analysis is needed on those variables or not.

Quote-Unquote

> The goal is to turn data into information and information into insight.
>
> *~Carly Fiorina, ex-CEO of HP*

Different types of analysis based on variables include:

- **Univariate**
  - Analysis is the anlysis of one variable.
- **Bivariate**
  - Analysis is between two variables to determine their relationship.

- **Multivariate**

◆ Analysis is of multiple outcome variables.

- **Principal Components**

◆ Analysis is done to convert correlated variables into a smaller number of uncorrelated variables.

The most commonly used visual representation tools include:

MS Excel, MapR, Microsoft Power BI, Google Chart, Qlik Infogram and Tableau.

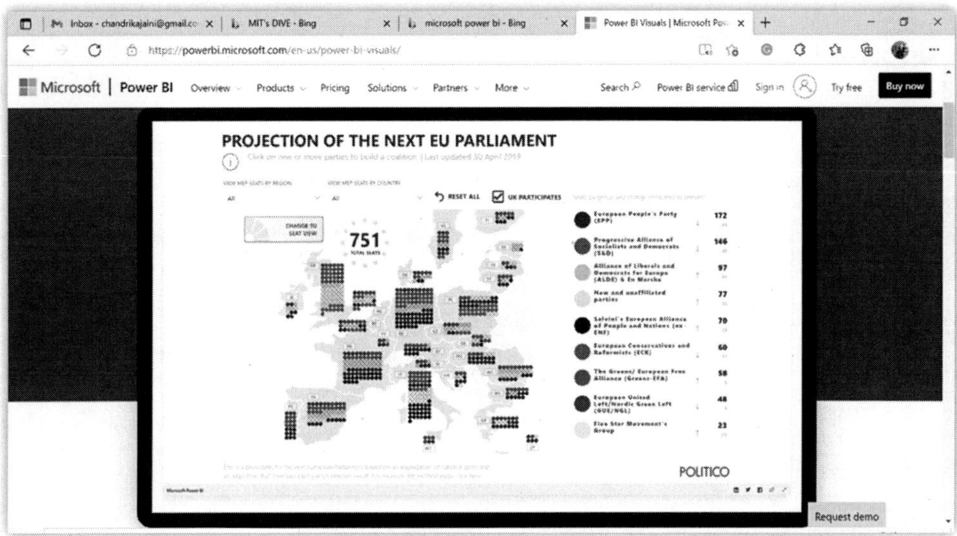

Figure 3.9: Power BI

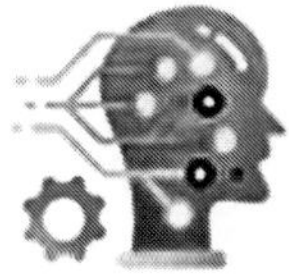

WHY IS DATA VISUALISATION IMPORTANT?

Good algorithms are produced only when they are trained using good quality data. Using bad quality data results in misleading outcomes.

Therefore, it is essential to know the data sources and the process followed to collect the data. The data factors to look out for are as follows:

Quality Check

It is essential to check the quality of data before analysing it. As mentioned earlier, the bad quality of data may result in poor or misleading outcomes. Hence, it is essential to collect data which is relevant and acquired from reliable sources.

Figure 3.10: Quality data is needed

Complete Data Collection

Another factor to consider while collecting data is to check if the complete set of data is collected. Fractured data again may result in wrong analysis.

Data Format

Once the data is collected, it should be placed in a proper format to make the analysis more result-oriented. For example, data collected in a text file cannot be analysed till it is placed in software like MS Excel.

Figure 3.11: Data placed in proper format

Goal Specification

Once the relevant data is collected, we should determine the insights we wish to get from the data. Knowing what to look for in the data is an important step in the data analysis cycle. Unless one knows what specifically they are looking for in the data, they won't achieve their goal.

Figure 3.12: Goal specification is essential

TYPES OF ANALYSIS

After the goal is set and relevant data is collected, the next step involves choosing which type of data analysis to do. There are three statistical analysis techniques that are most commonly used. Let us look at them.

a. **Regression Analysis:** It helps to find out the relationships between variables in the data. It helps to specify the independent (predictor variables) and dependent (response variables) nature of the variables. For example, scientists may use regression analysis to measure the effect of fertilizer and water on

Figure 3.13: Regression analysis

crop yields. Here, fertilizers and water are the independent variables, whereas crop yield is the dependent variable.

ACTIVITY 3.2

Give two more example situations where regression analysis could be used.

____

____

____

____

b. **Cohort Analysis:** It compares data related to groups and cohorts. For example, the data professional can create a date-wise cohort of patients when they visit a dentist. Thereafter, he/ she can study the visiting trends of cohorts from different periods in time to determine whether the quality of the average acquired patient is increasing or decreasing over time.

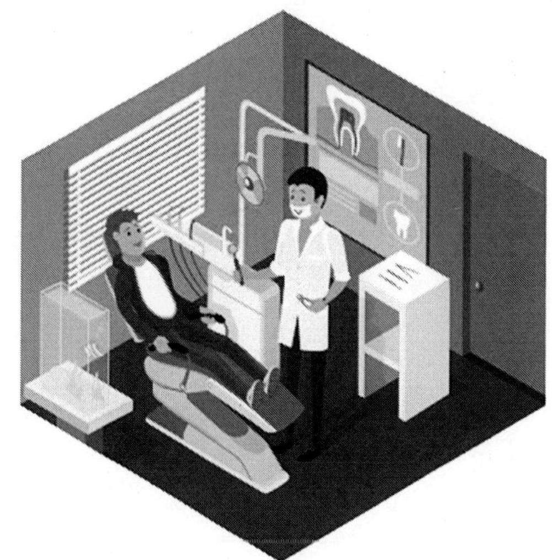

Figure 3.14: Cohort analysis

c. **Predictive Analysis:** It predicts future possibilities based on the datasets collected earlier. It is also used to determine risk assessments. For example, weather forecasting websites analyse weather patterns in an area using satellite imagery and historical data and predict the weather up to 30 days in advance.

Figure 3.15: Predictive analysis

Outcome Expectations

This step involves identifying the end-users of the analysis of data collected. What are their expectations? How tech-savvy are they? Whether they will be able to interpret the reports that are generated after data analysis? This helps in detailing and documentation of the outcomes expected. For example, a non-technical person may not understand complex technical reports, or a technical person may require a more complex report which could deliver more insights. Therefore, the reports generated should be understandable to the target users.

VISUALISATION TOOLS

Analysed data requires proper visualisation. The popular adage 'a picture tells a thousand words' holds true in the case of data analysis. Which of the two pictures below is easier to understand? The first one, isn't it? Visualising any kind of data leads to better and easier understanding.

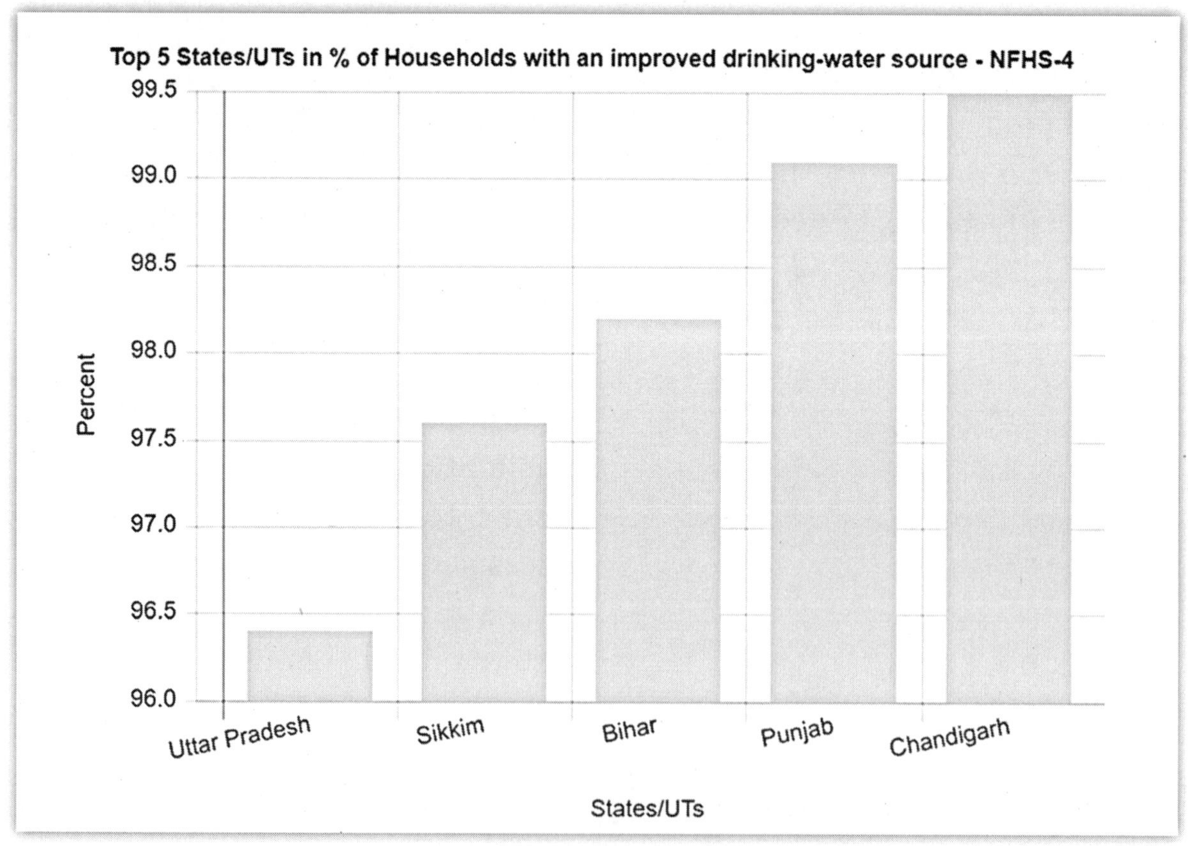

Figure 3.16: Visualsed data

India/States/UTs	Survey	Area	Age 6 Years And Above Who Ever Attended School (%)	Household Profile - Population Below Age 15 Years (%)	Of The Total Population (Females Per 1000 Males)	Born In The Last Five Years (Females Per 1000 Males)	Under Age 5 Years Whose Birth Was Registered (%)	Household Profile - Households With Electricity (%)	Households With An Improved Drinking-Water Source (%)	Profile - Househol Using Improved Sanitation Facility (%
Bihar	NFHS-3	Total	39.4	43.8	1083	893	5.8	27.7	96.1	14.6
Rajasthan	NFHS-3	Total	43.9	38.9	957	847	16.4	66.1	81.8	19.3
Jharkhand	NFHS-3	Total	46.3	39.5	1022	1091	9.1	40.2	57	15.1
Uttar Pradesh	NFHS-3	Total	50.2	42.3	987	922	7.1	42.8	93.7	20.6
Telangana	NFHS-4	Rural	50.4	25.1	1035	865	76.5	97.2	75.6	38.9
Madhya Pradesh	NFHS-3	Total	52	37.3	961	960	29.7	71.4	74.2	18.7
Rajasthan	NFHS-4	Rural	52	32.6	989	899	62.5	88.4	83.3	35.6

Powered by visualize. data.gov

Figure 3.17: Data in a table

Source: *https://data.gov.in/major-indicator/households-improved-drinking-water-source*

Once the data is collected and analysed, the next step involves selecting an appropriate visualisation tool. One can select from various charts and graphs available. Some types include:

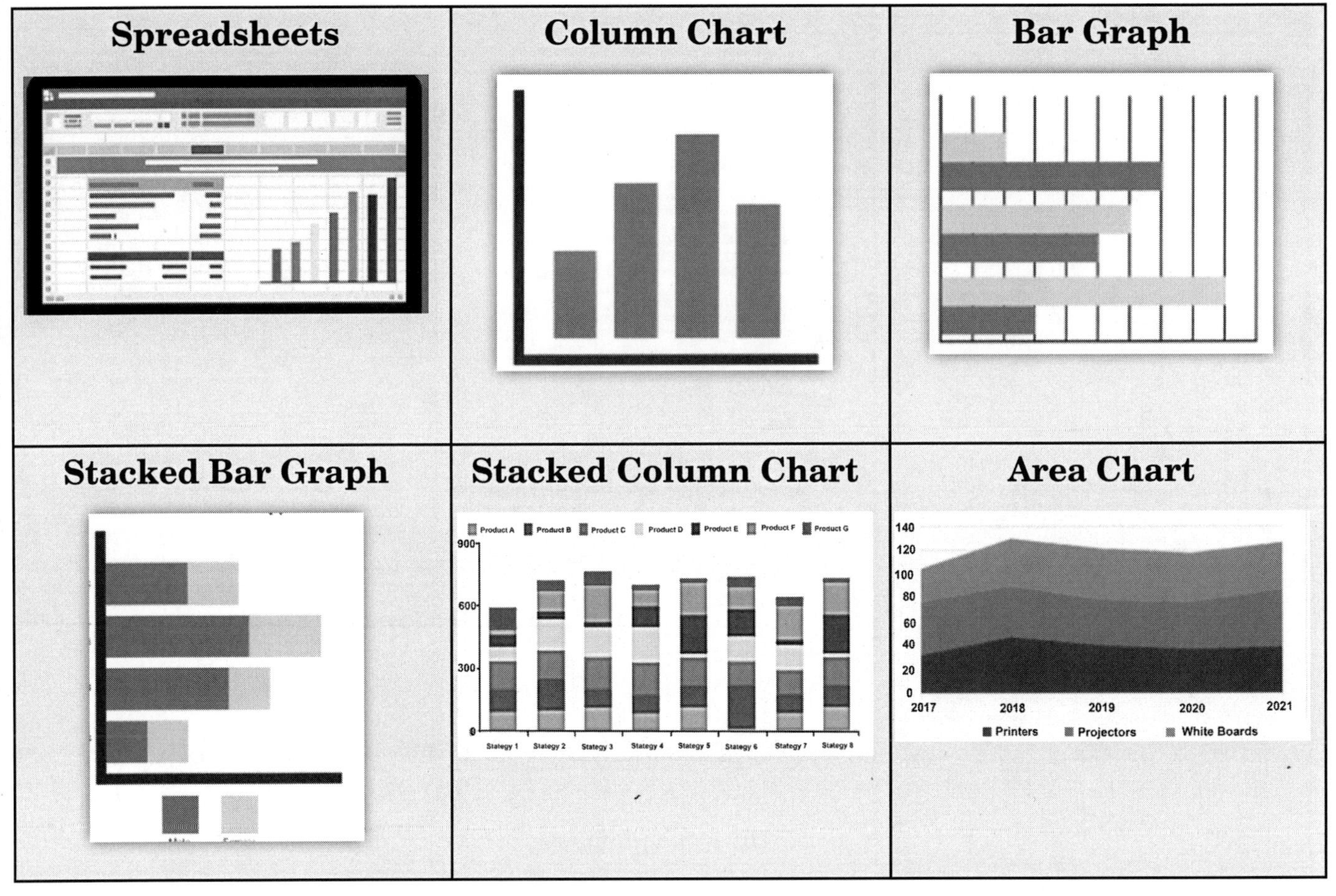

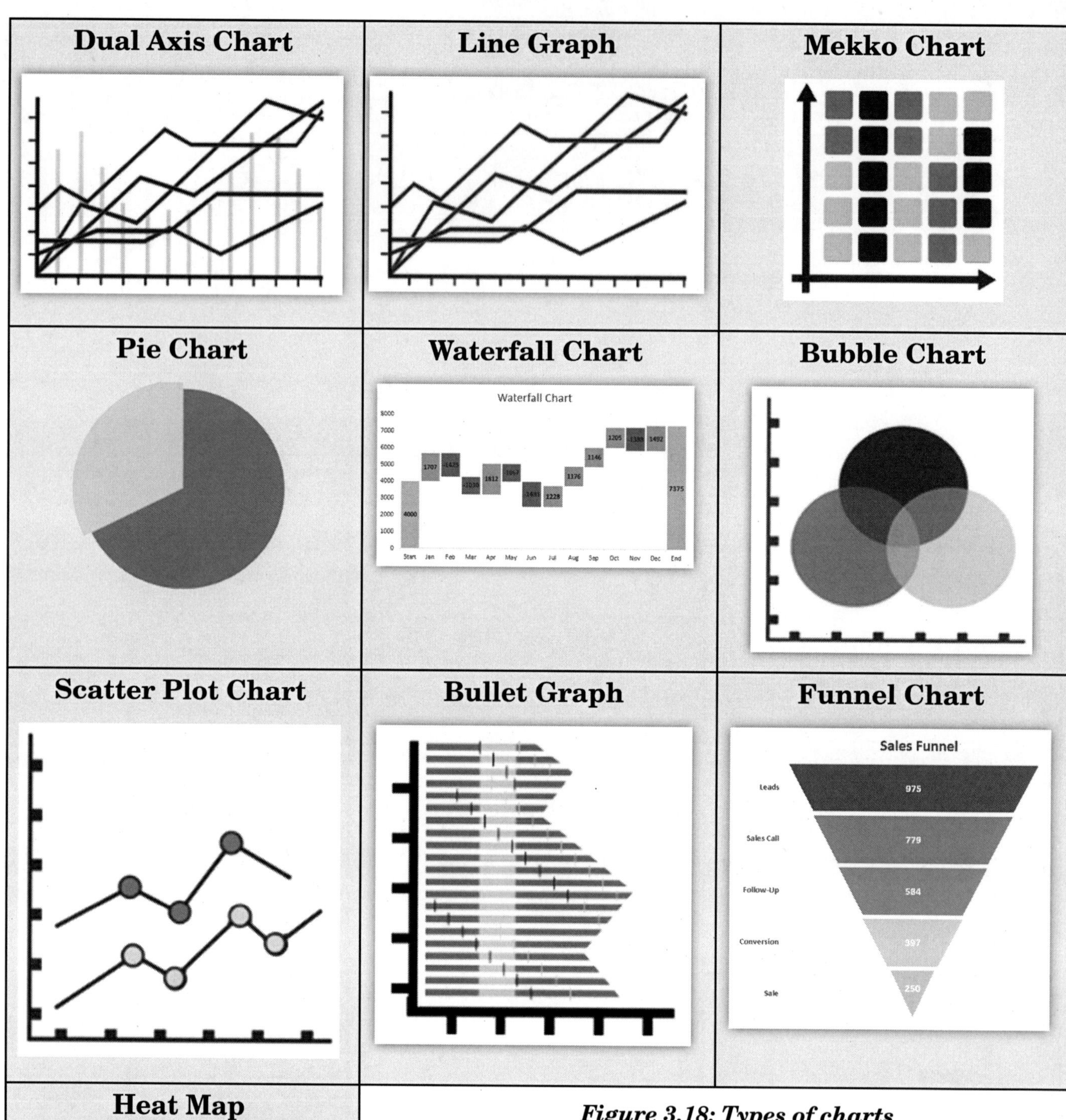

Figure 3.18: Types of charts

Apart from these, various types of tables and diagrams are also used for data visualisation and exploration.

ACTIVITY 3.3

Find out and write the names of any three data visualisation software.

____

____

These charting tools allow a quick and straightforward view of the most relevant features of a dataset. This step helps the analyst to identify the important variables in the dataset. By displaying data through various types of charts, for example, bar charts, scatter and density plots, etc., data scientists can study the variables and relationships between them. This helps them decide if further analysis is needed on those variables or not.

Let us discuss some of them:

Line Chart

A line chart displays information as a series of data points called 'markers' connected by line segments. These are straight lines. Observe the example chart.

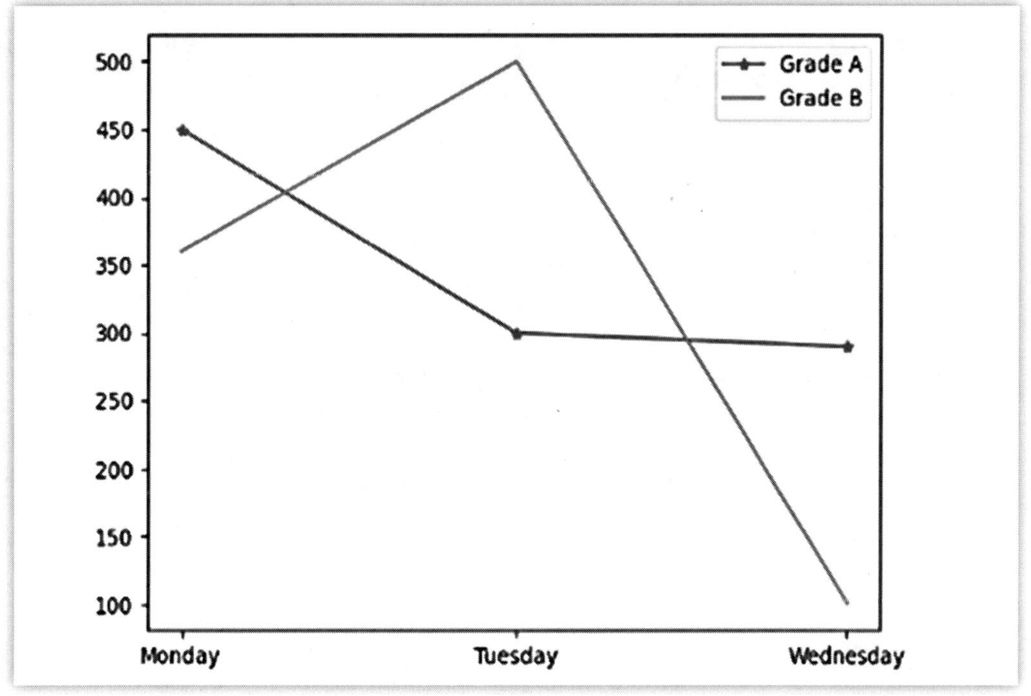

Figure 3.19: Line chart

Bar Chart

A bar chart is a graph that displays data in rectangular bars, either vertically or horizontally. Let us look at an example chart.

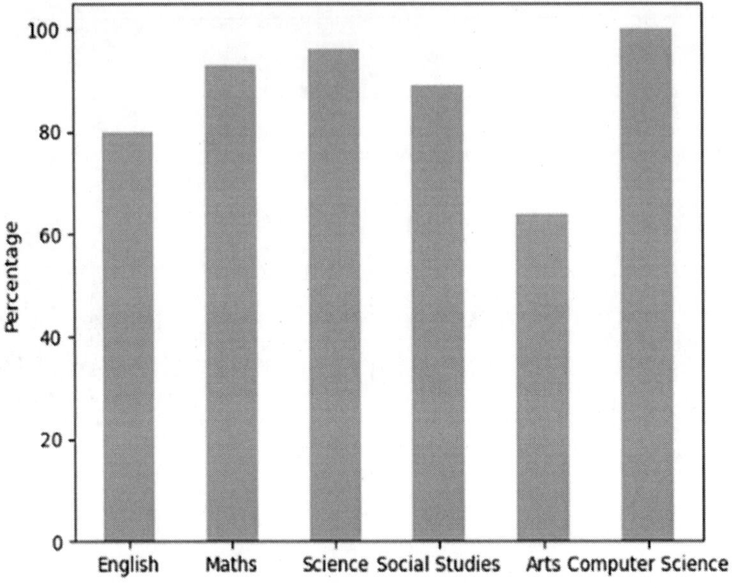

Figure 3.20: Bar chart

Scatter Plots

A dot in a scatter plot represents each value in the data set. This type of plot displays data that doesn't have continuity. Look at the scatter plot below.

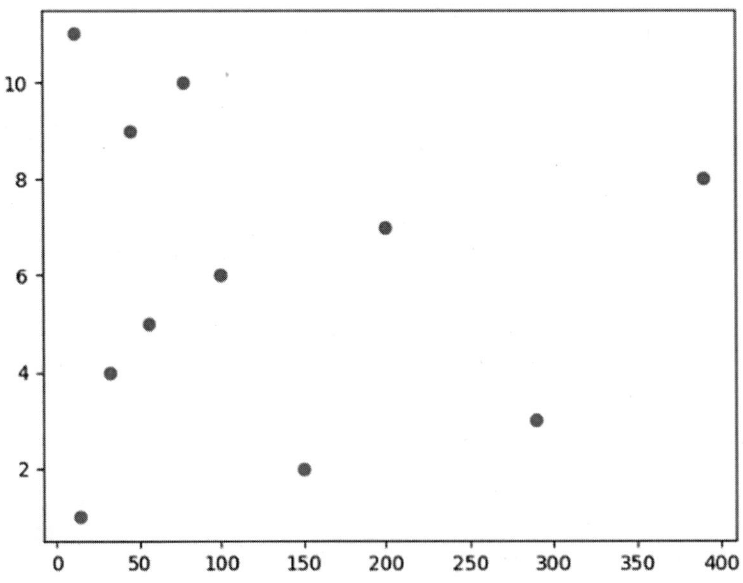

Figure 3.21: Scatter plotting

Here is another example with two different datasets, each having different coloured dots.

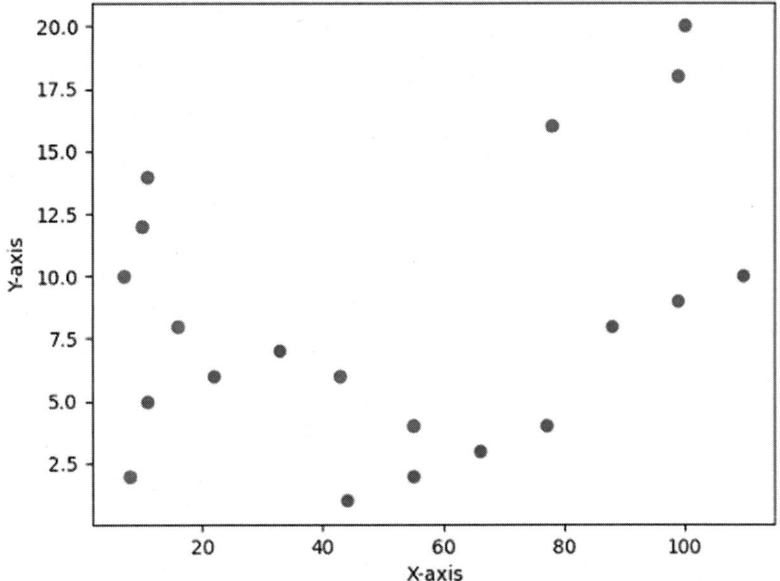

Figure 3.22: Scatter plot with two datasets

Histogram

It resembles a bar graph and represents the probable distribution of continuous numerical data. The parameters of the function include- variable and bin, which is the range of values. The bins are consecutive, non-overlapping intervals of a variable. Following is a histogram of the age group of people who went to vote. The bins are defined as follows- 18-25, 26-40, 41-60, 61-75 and 76-110. The histogram shows the number of people falling in this range.

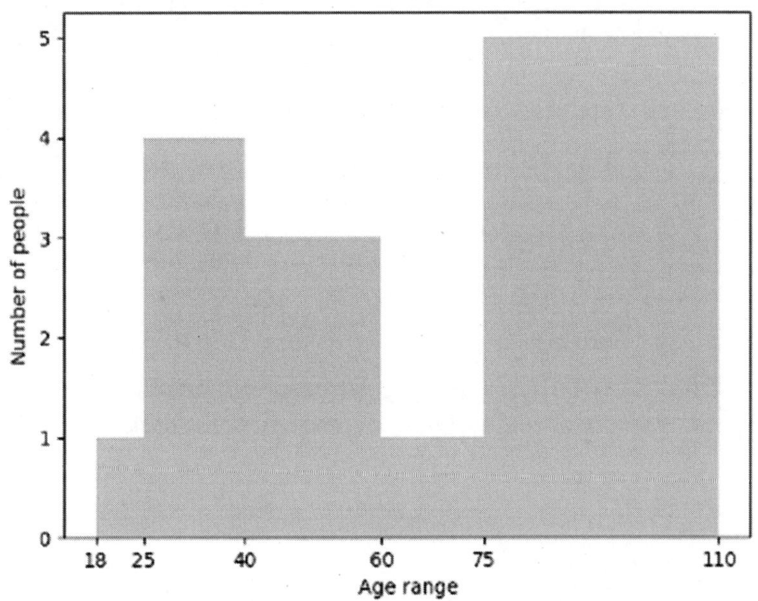

Figure 3.23: Histogram

POINTS TO REMEMBER

- The life cycle of data science passes through various stages.
- Project definition defines the project requirements.
- After the business problem is identified, data related to it is collected.
- Data scientists use software to gather and place data in a format which could later be analysed.
- The collected data in tables is stored in different formats by the data scientists.
- Data is visually represented to give clear information to the users.
- Most organisations use automated visualisation charting tools because these allow a quick and straightforward view of the most relevant features of a dataset.
- The most commonly used visual representation tools include MS Excel, MapR, Microsoft Power BI, Google Chart, Qlik Infogram and Tableau.
- Good algorithms are produced only when they are trained by using good quality data.
- It is essential to check the quality of data before analysing it.
- Once the data is collected, it should be placed in a proper format to make the analysis more result-oriented.
- Three statistical analysis techniques are most commonly used: Regression analysis, Cohort analysis, and Predictive analysis.
- Analysed data requires proper visualisation.
- By displaying data through various types of charts, for example, bar charts, scatter and density plots, etc., data scientists can study the variables and relationships between them.

GLOSSARY

- **Project definition:** It defines the project requirements.
- **Data collection:** It is when the data professionals collect the data.
- **Data sources:** These are the sources from which data is gathered.
- **Data visualisation:** It involves displaying data in graphs and charts.
- **Univariate analysis:** It is the analysis of one variable.
- **Bivariate:** This analysis is between two variables to determine their relationship.
- **Multivariate:** This analysis is of multiple outcome variables.
- **Principal components:** This analysis is done to convert correlated variables into a smaller number of uncorrelated variables.
- **Regression analysis:** This analysis helps to find out the relationships between variables in the data.
- **Cohort analysis:** This analysis compares data related to groups and cohorts.
- **Predictive analysis:** This analysis predicts future possibilities based on the earlier datasets; it is also used to determine risk assessments.
- **Line chart:** It displays information as a series of data points called 'markers' connected by line segments; these are straight lines.
- **Bar chart:** This graph displays data in rectangular bars, either vertically or horizontally.
- **Scatter plot:** This graph displays data which doesn't have continuity.
- **Histogram:** It resembles a bar graph and represents the probable distribution of continuous numerical data.

EXERCISE

Multiple choice questions.

1. How many stages are there in a data cycle?

   a. Ten ☐ b. Four ☐

   c. Five ☐ d. Seven ☐

2. Digital records of organisations are an example of which data collection source?

   a. Offline ☐ b. Online ☐

   c. Personal ☐ d. Sensitive ☐

3. Which of the following statement is false?

   a. Raw data is easy to comprehend. ☐

   b. Raw data is difficult to comprehend. ☐

   c. Raw data needs to be formatted. ☐

   d. Raw data is collected from various sources. ☐

4. Which of the following statement is true?

   a. Bar chart is a graph that displays data in rectangular bars. ☐

   b. Pie chart is a graph that displays data in rectangular bars. ☐

   c. Scatter plot is a graph that displays data in rectangular bars. ☐

   d. Line chart is a graph that displays data in rectangular bars. ☐

5. Most organisations use automated visualisation charting tools because-

   a. it is a smarter way of presenting data. ☐

   b. they display the most relevant features of the dataset. ☐

   c. these allow a quick and straightforward view of the dataset. ☐

   d. all of the above ☐

6. Which of the following is one of the data factors to check while collecting data?

a. Data sharing ☐ b. Data format ☐

c. Data privacy ☐ d. Data availability ☐

7. Regression analysis helps us to find–

a. relationship between offline and online sources. ☐

b. relationship between project and data techniques ☐

c. relationships between variables in the data ☐

d. relationship between collection and organisation of data ☐

8. The predictive analysis does future risk assessments.

a. True ☐ b. False ☐

9. Which of the following helps in detailing and documenting of expectations?

a. Outline Expectations ☐ b. Outcome Expectations ☐

c. Online Expectations ☐ d. Outbound Expectations ☐

10. What is the name for a series of data points in a line chart?

a. Markers ☐ b. Makers ☐

c. Matters ☐ d. Mappers ☐

11. Which format of data will be easiest to analyse?

a. Text file ☐ b. Image file ☐

c. Sound file ☐ d. Spreadsheet ☐

12. A bar chart is a graph that displays data in rectangular bars, either vertically or horizontally.

a. True ☐ b. False ☐

13. How is the value in the dataset represented in scatter plots?

a. Bars ☐ b. Sections ☐

c. Dots ☐ d. Lines ☐

14. Which of the following is a visual representation tool?

a. MapR ☐ b. Mapr ☐

c. mapR ☐ d. MApr ☐

15. Histogram represents what kind of data?

a. Probable distribution of broken data ☐

b. Probable distribution of unrelated data ☐

c. Probable distribution of continuous numerical data ☐

d. Probable distribution of overlapping data. ☐

16. Visualising any kind of data leads to better and easier understanding.

a. True ☐ b. False ☐

17. Which of the following is a statistical analysis technique?

a. Cognizant Analysis ☐ b. Captive Analysis ☐

c. Correct Analysis ☐ d. Cohort Analysis ☐

Answer the following questions in short (100 words).

1. List the stages of the data science life cycle.

____

____

____

____

2. What is Project Definition?

____

____

____

____

3. What is meant by data source? Give two examples.

4. Define bivariate.

5. Mention two data factors to check for collecting quality data.

6. Where do most organisations such as banks, schools, hospitals, travel agencies, etc. store their data?

7. Explain outcome expectations.

8. Name a few data visualisation tools available in the market.

9. Name the three types of data analysis.

10. Explain analysis by principal components.

11. What is a line chart?

12. What kind of data does scatter plots display?

13. What is the difference between regression analysis and cohort analysis?

14. Give an example of predictive analysis.

15. Name at least five types of charts and graphs.

16. What is a histogram? Explain.

Answer in detail (150 words).

1. Explain data collection.

2. What are the types of analysis based on variables?

3. Why is data visualisation important? Explain with at least three reasons.

4. What are visualisation tools? Explain two tools.

5. Explain the bar chart with an example.

HOTS

Higher Order Thinking Skills

Saraswati believes that it is important to interact with the end-users before choosing data visualisation tools. What do you think? Justify your answer.

Applied Project

Start doing jumping-jacks from Sunday. Record the number of continuous jumps you could do each day. Do it for a week, from Sunday to Saturday. Now, take a graph paper and create a:

- bar graph to display jumps on each day.
- pie chart to show the percentage contribution of jumps on each day to the total jumps made.

Alternately, you can also create graphs online at the following URL:

https://datacopia.com/#/Data

We created one using sample data.

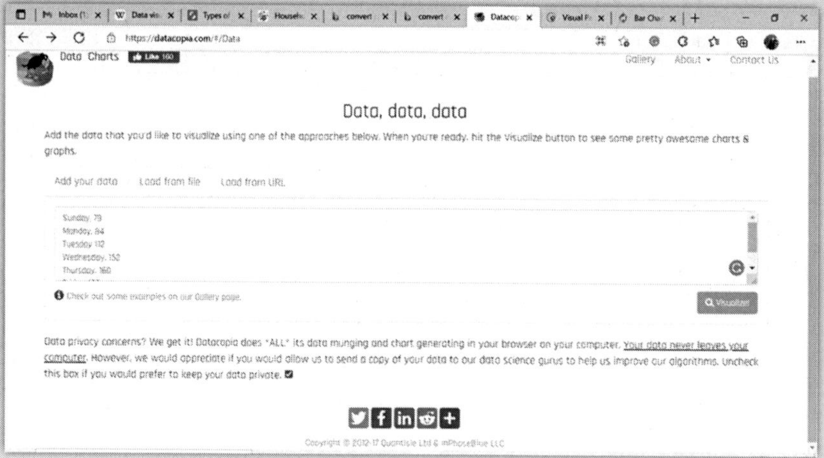

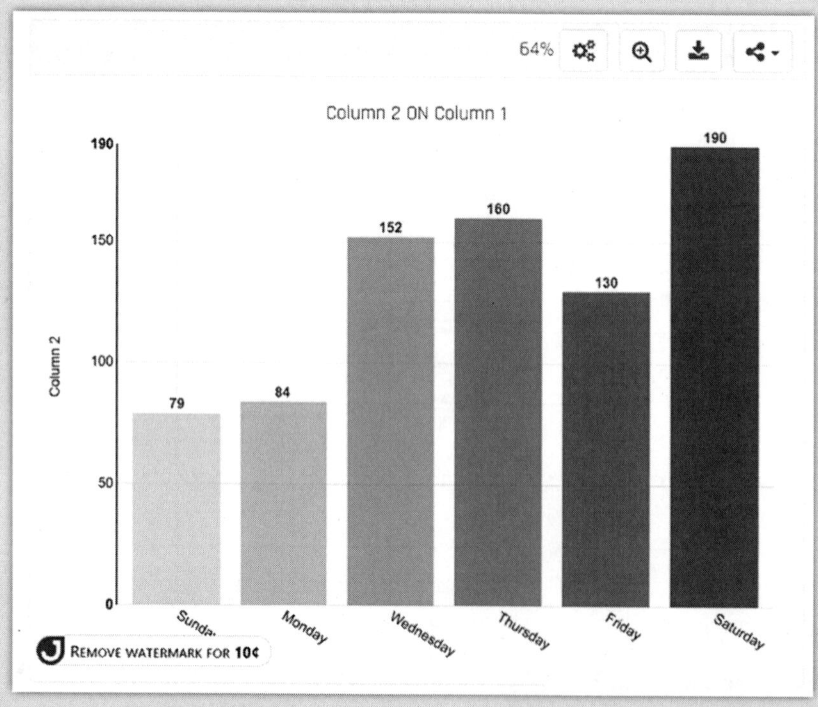

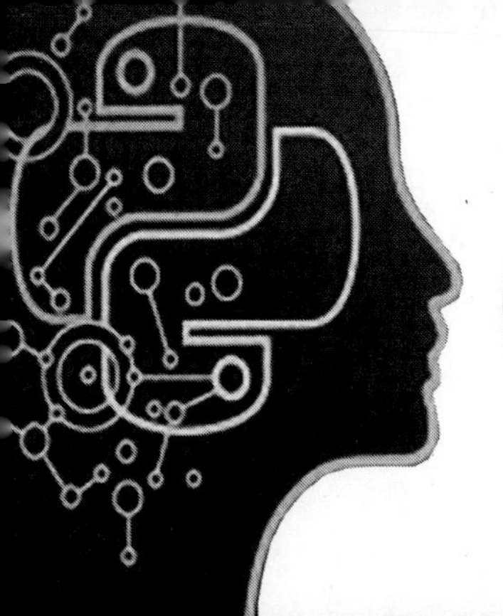

4 Data Science and AI

OBJECTIVES

After studying this chapter, you should be able to understand:

- Applications of data science
  - Analytics on text data
  - Analytics on image data
- Overview of AI

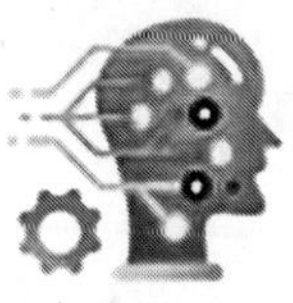

DATA SCIENCE APPLICATIONS

Data Science applications are helping businesses to grow exponentially. This particular domain of Artificial Intelligence is widespread. It is everywhere, from homes to rover on Mars.. It is changing our life in general. Data analysis has led to further understanding of text and images. Data is gathered, cleaned, and analysed to give insights and make predictions. It has given rise to many new professions too, as learned in one of the earlier chapters.

Figure 4.1: Data is everywhere

Data analysis is performed on:

- Text, and
- Images

TEXT DATA ANALYSIS

Text data, when collected, most probably is unorganised and unstructured. When high-quality information is sieved from a large volume of text, it is called **text data analysis** or **text mining**. There are methods to analyse the unstructured text, the major one being **NLP (Natural Language Processing)**. It is an area of AI concerned with the interactions between computer and human languages. Algorithms in NLP try to read, interpret and understand human languages.

Figure 4.2: NLP works with human languages

Examples of text analysis include:

Automatic summarisation: These days, even a small entity has loads of information available on it. Information overload has become a problem when a person needs specific information on something from a knowledge base. Automatic summarisation follows the 3C rule- crisp, concise and cohesive information imparting. It avoids redundancy from multiple resources. It not only provides crisp information but also understands the emotional meanings within the information. An example is collecting data from a social media site. Another example is providing an overview of a news item.

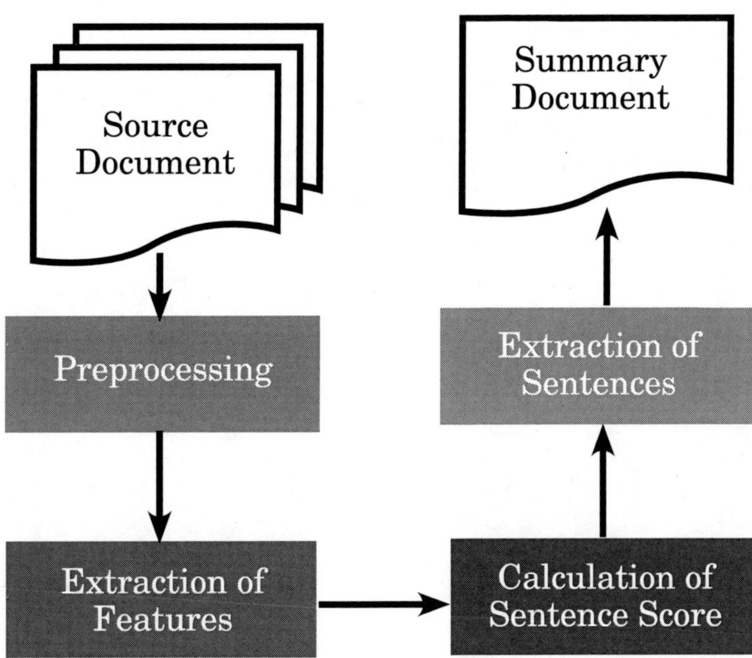

Figure 4.3: Step by step text summarization

Text classification: This application of NLP assigns labels so that information is appropriately organised. An example is spam detection, where the input is an email or text message, which is analysed and labelled as spam or not spam.

Virtual assistants: Smart virtual assistants like Amazon's Alexa, Apple's Siri and Microsoft's Cortana use voice recognition and inference techniques of NLP to provide useful responses. They not only detect our speech but also understand it, thus help us do our tasks.

Figure 4.4: Virtual assistants

Chatbots: One of the most common applications of Natural Language Processing is a chatbot. These are mainly used to provide customer service. Chatbots are utilised in lieu of interacting with humans. The interaction with a chatbot could be through text or via speech to text or vice versa. We can call them **conversation simulators**.

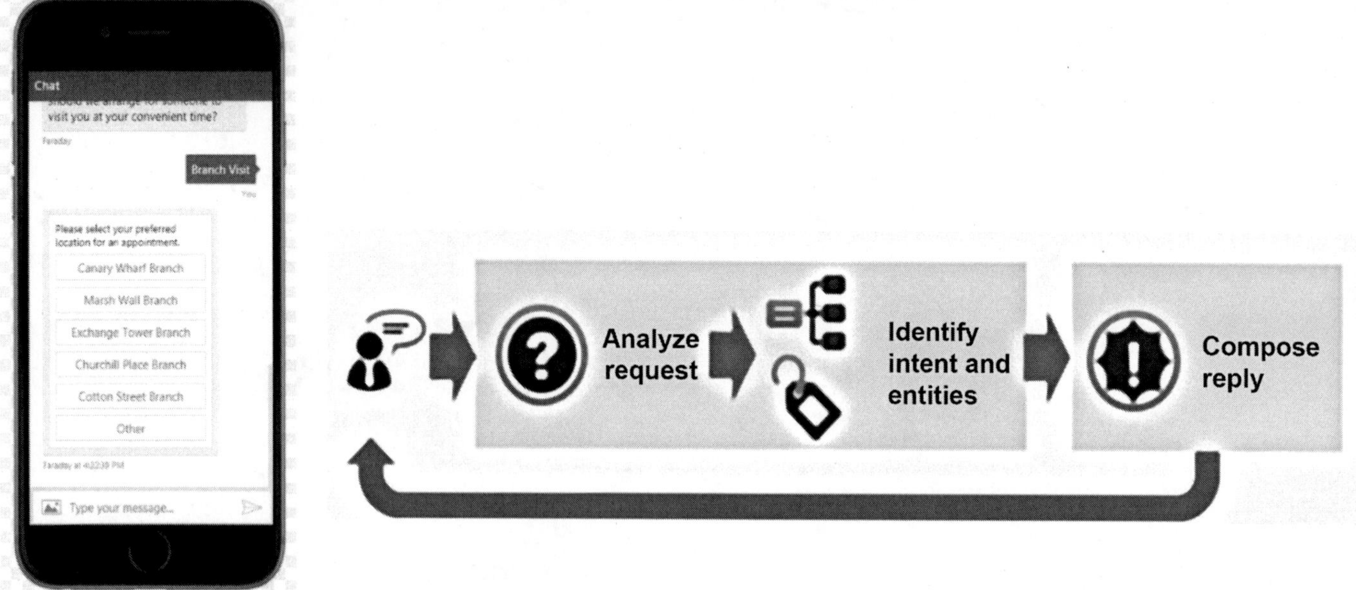

Figure 4.5: How a chatbot works

There are a lot of chatbots available online, and some of the best ones are-

a. **Endurance**: Chats with patients who have Alzheimer's or Dementia.

b. **U-Report**: Helps marginalised communities be heard.

c. **MedWhat:** Makes faster medical diagnosis.

IMAGE DATA ANALYSIS

We know that while humans absorb their surroundings using sense organs, computers do the same through inputs. We see things through our eyes. Intelligent machines 'see' things through digital images.

Intelligent machines see and understand digital images and videos and then make predictions or decisions. The entire process involves the following steps:

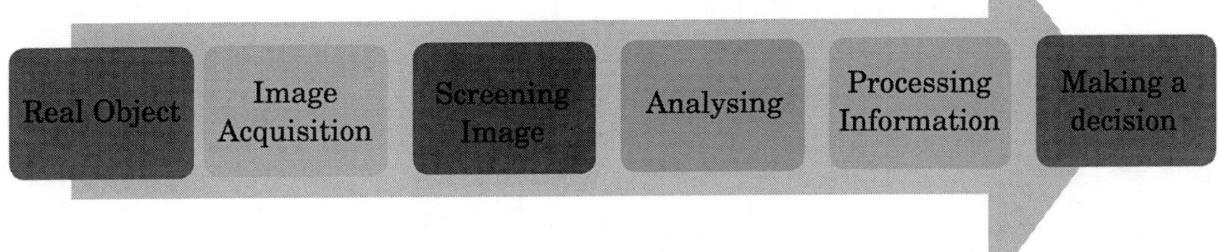

Figure 4.6: Image data analysis

The main objective of this domain of AI is to teach machines to collect information from pixels.

ACTIVITY 4.1

- Visit the following URL:

https://emojiscavengerhunt.withgoogle.com/

Emoji Scavenger Hunt

- It is a Google experiment named Emoji Scavenger Hunt.
- It is a game built with Machine Learning that uses your device's camera to capture pictures. It then uses a neural network to try and guess what it is seeing.
- Play the game and answer the following questions.

- Were you able to play it on a phone/ tablet successfully?

  ____

- Did you gain any points?

  ____

- What was the strategy that you implemented?

  ____

- Was the device able to identify all the items you showed it?

  ____

- Next, alter the light in the room and play the game again. Was there any change in the results due to this action?

  ____

Let us look at some of the applications of image data analysis:

Facial recognition: It is an application that helps to identify or verify an individual's identity using their face in real-time or photos and videos. It is used in many areas, some of which are mentioned below.

- Unlocking smartphones and computer devices.
- Scanning visitors through security cameras at homes.
- Inbuilt cameras in smart locks.
- Scanning commuters at airports.
- Identifying shoplifters at departmental stores.
- Tracking customers' movements and patterns through stores.

Figure 4.7: Customer tracking

- Identifying criminals by the police from a safe distance.
- Identifying fraudsters at banks.
- Taking attendance of students in educational institutions and many more.

Search by image: It uses image analysis techniques to search for data using an image. It compares the different features of the input image to the database of images and gives us the search result.

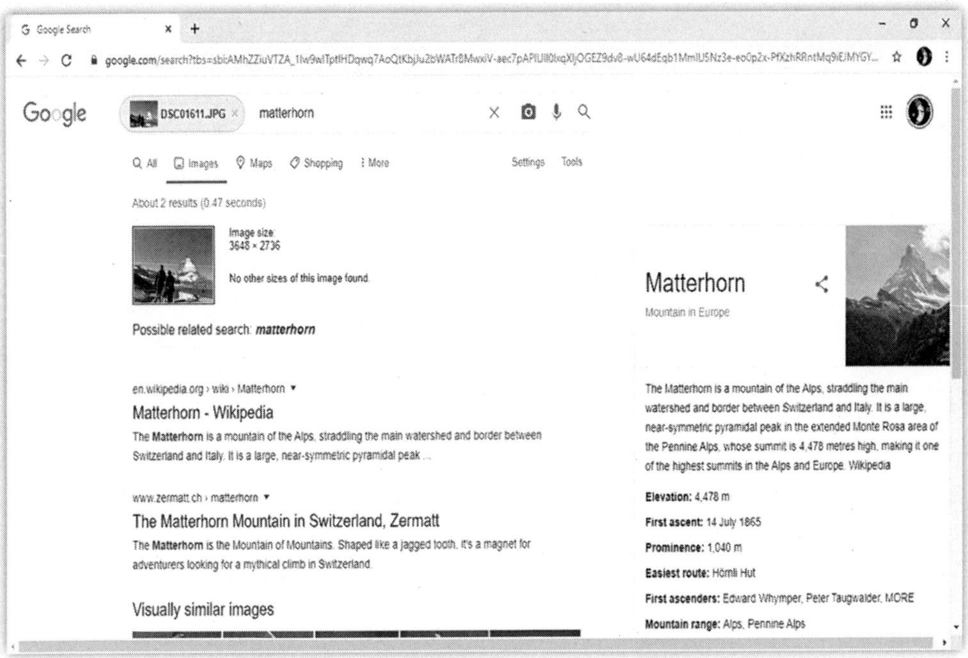

Figure 4.8: Search by image

Computers are everywhere today. It is inconceivable to carry out our daily lives while not employing a computer in some way or the other. We tend to use computers all the time unwittingly, like video games, cars, online banking, televisions, mobile phones and even toys. That is why computers must become more intelligent to make our lives better.

What is the first thing we think of on hearing the phrase, "*Artificial Intelligence*"? Perhaps Sci-fi movies like '*The Terminator*', '*The Avengers*' or '*iRobot*'? Ever since the invention of the computer, science fiction has made us believe in the likelihood of super-intelligent computers. Technology has developed at tremendous speed within the past few decades and has integrated AI into our lives. Typical examples are GPS Navigators, Universal remote controls, Amazon Alexa and Apple Siri.

Figure 4.9: GPS navigator

Figure 4.10: Universal remote controls

Artificial Intelligence, or AI, is a field of computer science that tries to simulate characteristics of human intelligence or senses. These comprise learning, reasoning, and adapting.

The computer programs written explicitly for this purpose perform tasks such as recognising and comprehending human speech, developing simulations, and analysing an immense amount of data to derive useful information.

Figure 4.11: AI- a vital branch of computer science

AI forms a vital branch of computer science and is widely researched across government and private organisations worldwide for providing solutions to real-life problems. AI systems are now in routine use in economics, medicine, engineering and the military and embedded within common home appliances like televisions, refrigerators, dishwashers and many more. There is a tremendous potential for this technology that is still maturing and will embed in our daily lives one day.

Types of AI

There are three types of Artificial Intelligence:

- **Artificial Narrow Intelligence (ANI)**, which has a narrow range of abilities. It mainly focuses on one problem and one solution. Examples are Siri, Alexa and Cortana.
- **Artificial General Intelligence (AGI)**, which is at par with human capabilities.
- **Artificial Super Intelligence (ASI)** will be more capable than the human brain and surpasses human capabilities.

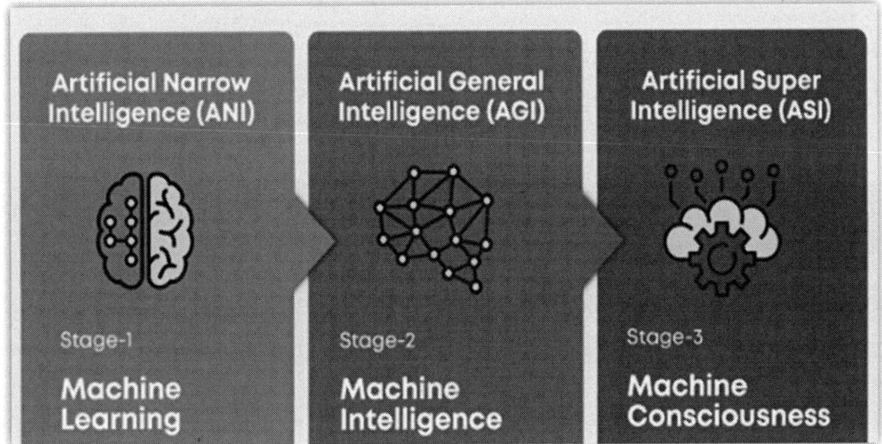

Figure 4.12: Types of AI

The timeline of the three types of Artificial Intelligence is projected as follows:

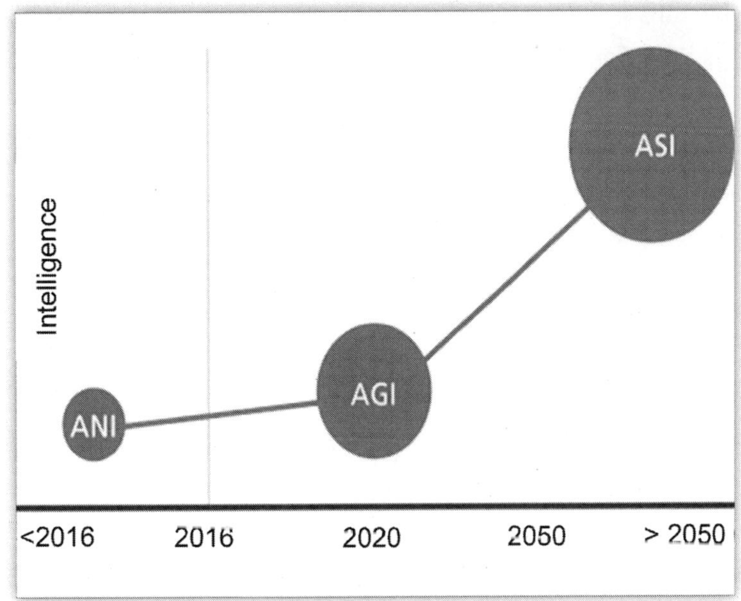

Figure 4.13: Timeline of AI

AI, ML, DL

At times, the terms Artificial Intelligence, Machine Learning and Deep Learning may mean the same to novices. However, there are marked differences between the three.

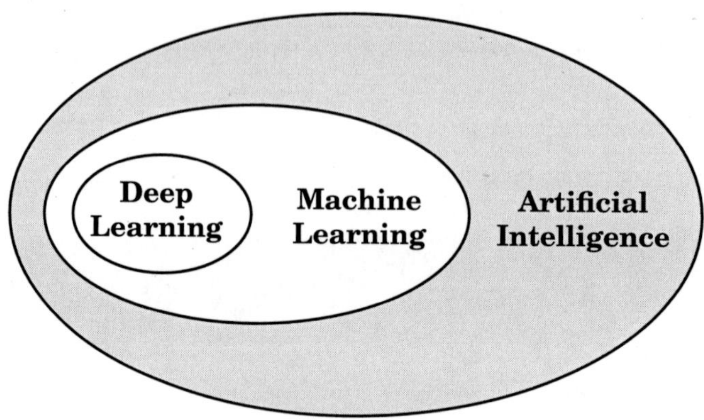

Figure 4.14: AI, ML, DL

As we can deduce from the above given figure 4.14, Machine Learning is a subset of Artificial Intelligence and Deep Learning is a subset of Machine Learning. Let us learn about all three.

Artificial Intelligence (AI)

Quote-Unquote

According to NITI Aayog- National Strategy for Artificial Intelligence:
"AI refers to the ability of machines to perform cognitive tasks like thinking, perceiving, learning, problem-solving and decision making. Initially conceived as a technology that could mimic human intelligence, AI has evolved in ways that far exceed its original conception. With incredible advances made in data collection, processing and computation power, intelligent systems can now be deployed to take over a variety of tasks, enable connectivity and enhance productivity."

Therefore, we can infer that Artificial Intelligence, or AI, is a field of computer science that tries to simulate characteristics of human intelligence or senses. These comprise learning, reasoning, and adapting.

AI is made of three parts:

A **data set** is a collection of data, which can be in any form- numbers, characters, letters, images, video and audio, and even views. A data set defines how people and the world around them behave with respect to each other.

An **algorithm** is a set of instructions which follows the IPO (Input-Processing-Output) cycle in order to do a task.

The **prediction** is the probability of outcomes that could arise when an algorithm is executed. For example, our email service provider learns to identify spam by looking at lots and lots of examples which we had earlier marked as spam. It predicts when shown a new email, whether it's spam or not.

Machine Learning (ML)

Machine Learning is a subset of Artificial Intelligence and is concerned with designing and developing algorithms that allow computers to evolve behaviours based on experimental data. The idea behind machine learning is to make machines self-reliant in learning to provide accurate outcomes/ predictions or make correct decisions.

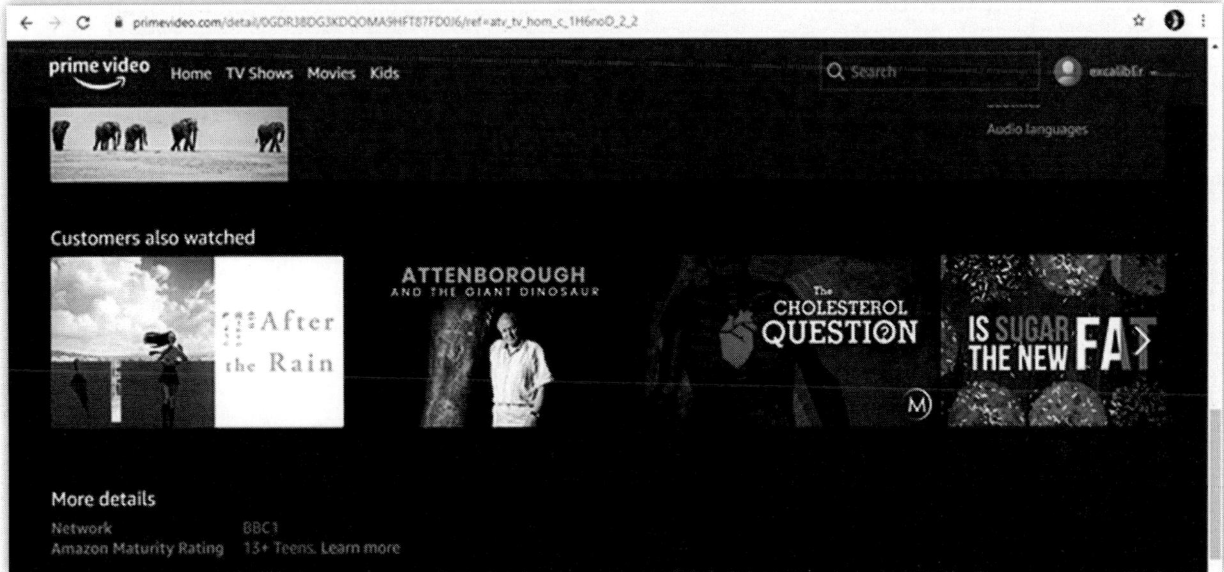

Figure 4.15: Amazon Prime Video

Netflix and Amazon's Prime Video use ML algorithms to predict our likes.

ACTIVITY 4.2

- Write the names of two more service providers that you think use recommendation algorithms.

____

____

Deep Learning (DL)

Deep Learning is a subset of Machine Learning. Here, machines are taught to self-design and generate algorithms. Algorithms in Deep Learning are inspired by the structure of a human brain and use complex multi-layered neural networks. It is the most advanced form of Artificial Intelligence.

POINTS TO REMEMBER

- Data Science applications are helping businesses to grow exponentially.
- Data is gathered, cleaned, and analysed to give insights and make predictions.
- Algorithms in NLP try to read, interpret and understand human languages.
- Automatic summarisation follows the 3C rule: crisp, concise and cohesive information imparting.
- Smart virtual assistants like Amazon's Alexa, Apple's Siri and Microsoft's Cortana use voice recognition and inference techniques of NLP to provide useful responses.
- Chatbots are mainly used in lieu of interacting with humans.
- Intelligent machines see and understand digital images and videos and then make predictions or decisions.

- AI forms a vital branch of computer science and is widely researched across government and private organisations worldwide for providing solutions to real-life problems.
- At times, the terms Artificial Intelligence, Machine Learning and Deep Learning may mean the same to novices. However, there are marked differences between the three.
- The idea behind machine learning is to make machines self-reliant in learning so that they can provide accurate outcomes/ predictions or make correct decisions.
- Algorithms in Deep Learning are inspired by the structure of a human brain and use complex multi-layered neural networks.

GLOSSARY

- **NLP (Natural language processing):** The area of AI concerned with the interactions between computer and human languages.
- **Facial recognition:** The application that helps to identify or verify an individual's identity using their face in real-time or photos and videos.
- **Search by image:** It uses image analysis techniques to search for data using an image.
- **Artificial intelligence:** The field of computer science that tries to simulate characteristics of human intelligence or senses- learning, reasoning, and adapting.
- **Artificial Narrow Intelligence (ANI):** It has narrow range of abilities and mainly focuses on one problem and one solution.
- **Artificial General Intelligence (AGI):** It is at par with human capabilities.
- **Artificial Super Intelligence (ASI):** It will be more capable than the human brain and surpass human capabilities.

- **Data set:** It is the collection of data, which can be in any form- numbers, characters, letters, images, video and audio, and even views.
- **Algorithm:** The set of instructions that follow the IPO (Input-Processing-Output) cycle to do a task.
- **Prediction:** It is the probability of outcomes that could arise when an algorithm is executed.
- **Machine learning (ML):** It is the subset of Artificial Intelligence and is concerned with designing and developing algorithms that allow computers to evolve behaviours based on experimental data.
- **Deep learning:** It is the subset of Machine Learning where machines are taught to self-design and generate algorithms.

EXERCISE

Multiple choice questions.

1. What do you mean by ML?

   a. Material Learning ☐ b. Machine Learning ☐

   c. Material Locating ☐ d. Machine Locating ☐

2. Data analysis is performed on which of the following?

   a. Text ☐ b. Systems ☐

   c. Audio files ☐ d. None of these ☐

3. Automatic Summarisation is an example of image analysis.

   a. True ☐ b. False ☐

4. Smart virtual assistants like Alexa use voice recognition and inference techniques of the following?

   a. MLP ☐ b. NLP ☐

c. NPL ☐ d. NIL ☐

5. What are chatbots called?

a. conversation stimulators ☐ b. conversation starters ☐

c. conversation mobilisers ☐ d. conversation initiators ☐

6. Intelligent machines 'see' things through images.

a. True ☐ b. False ☐

7. Scanning computers at airports use which kind of technology?

a. Sound mapping ☐ b. Facial Recognition ☐

c. Text analysis ☐ d. Table recognition ☐

8. Which of the following are not a type of AI?

i. Deep Intentionality

ii. Deep Intelligence

iii. Deep Learning

iv. Deep Adaptability

a. i, ii, iii. ☐ b. ii, iii, iv. ☐

c. i, ii, iv. ☐ d. i, iii, iv. ☐

9. Out of the types of AI, which one is at par with human capabilities?

a. Artificial Narrow Intelligence ☐

b. Artificial General Intelligence ☐

c. Artificial Deep Intelligence ☐

d. Artificial Super Intelligence ☐

10. Which of the following is not a type of AI?

a. Artificial Narrow Intelligence ☐

b. Artificial General Intelligence ☐

c. Artificial Deep Intelligence ☐

d. Artificial Super Intelligence ☐

11. ANI stands for which of the following?

a. Artificial Nero Intelligence ☐

b. Artificial Neutral Intelligence ☐

c. Artificial Normal Intelligence ☐

d. Artificial Narrow Intelligence ☐

12. Which one of the following is a subset of Machine Learning?

a. Deep Mapping ☐ b. Deep Imaging ☐

c. Deep Learning ☐ d. Deep Leaping ☐

13. An algorithm is a set of instructions that follows the IPO (Input-Processing-Output) cycle in order to do a task.

a. True ☐ b. False ☐

14. Cortana virtual assistant is a product of-

a. Amazon ☐ b. Apple ☐

c. Google ☐ d. Microsoft ☐

15. Which of the following is an e-commerce platform?

a. Wikipedia ☐ b. Cloud ☐

c. Amazon ☐ d. Google Search ☐

Answer the following questions in short (100 words).

1. What do we mean by AI?

____

____

____

____

2. What is text data analysis?

____

3. How do smart virtual assistants work?

4. Write two examples of best chatbots online?

5. What are the steps involved in analysing images by intelligent machines?

6. How many types of AI are there? What is ANI?

7. AI systems can learn and adapt as they make decisions. Comment.

8. What is the broad difference between AI, DL and ML?

9. What do we mean by prediction in AI?

10. What does NITI Aayog say about AI?

11. What are chatbots?

12. Explain natural language processing.

13. Write a short note on deep learning.

Answer in detail (150 words).

1. Write a short note on automatic summarisation.

2. What is image data analysis.

3. Explain the three types of AI.

4. Give an overview of AI.

5. Write a note on machine learning.

Higher Order Thinking Skills

Monica wants to enhance her selfies by adding objects like flowers, elf ears, tiara, etc. She makes use of filters in her app. Which technology do we think helps her achieve this?

____

____

____

____

____

____

____

Applied Project

One of the primary industries to benefit from Data Sciences is retail and e-commerce. It is used not just for forecasting sales of goods and services but also for predicting trends. In addition, these intelligent systems identify a potential customer base while optimising price structures for a particular section of consumers. Data Science is also applied to the feedback provided by the customers. This is called sentiment analysis.

Sentiment Analysis is where the input is a sentence/ phrase from social media feeds (like Facebook, Twitter, Instagram, LinkedIn, etc.), customer reviews (Amazon, Myntra, etc.), surveys, etc. It can also be in the form of emoji.

List some keywords and draw some emojis that could be used for sentiment analysis. Label those appropriately.

CHAPTERWISE SOLUTIONS

Chapter 1

Multiple choice questions.

1. a	2. d	3. b	4. a	5. b
6. a	7. a	8. d	9. a	10. b
11. a	12. a	13. c	14. c	15. d

Answer the following questions in short (100 words).

1. Data is the collection of information. A computer can record data as sounds, text, numbers, images, and videos.

   There are two types of data:

   a. **Quantitative data and Qualitative Data:** While quantitative data is factual and can be measured or counted, qualitative data is descriptive and cannot be counted.

   b. **Unstructured Data and Structured Data:** When data is jumbled up, it is called unstructured data. Organised data is called structured data.

2. **Unstructured data**

   - This is disorganised data.
   - It consists of all formats sounds, text, numbers, images and videos
   - Undefined
   - It cannot be analysed

   Structured Data

   - Organised data
   - Clearly defined
   - Can be analysed
   - Easily Searchable

3. The data source is the source from where data is collected. A tea seller can be a data source for the types of teas, the variety of tea recipes and even the types of customers. A lake can be a data source for aquatic plants and birds. A report card is a data source for performance in the class. A report card is a data source for performance in the class.

4. Data needs to be organised to be analysed. When data is collected initially it is in a jumbled form. This is unstructured data. It does not have the clarity required for analysis. It is just a collection of information raw and disorganised. When it is properly organised, it becomes structured and can be used for analysis.

5. Discrete and continuous data are quantitative data types. They are numeric in nature; they are different. Discrete data is both measurable and countable; Continuous data is only measurable. Discrete data has clear spaces. Continuous data can have any intervals.

6. A single data source can provide different types of data. For example, a lake can a data source for plants, birds and fishes. It can also be a data source for tourist traffic according to seasons.

7. The number of dishes that we order is discrete data, whereas the billed amount we pay is continuous data. Both discrete and continuous data are quantitative data types; they are numeric in nature but are different. Discrete data is both measurable and countable; continuous data is only measurable. Discrete data has clear spaces. Continuous data can have any intervals.

8. The first step is to place the data into a table. This table is called the database table. It contains only organised data in organised rows and columns. This data becomes clear, sensible and structured and ready to be analysed.

9. Spam filtering refers to the process of segregating emails in an inbox. It happens when some emails automatically go to the inbox while others end up in the spam folder. This is accomplished through data science. Spam filters (machine programs) are taught to recognise certain words in the mail, which classify them as spam. The program is trained using thousands of emails. After it gets trained, it segregates spam mails easily.

10. Biometrics refers to the physical features of a human being, which are unique in every person. These include finger and thumbprints, DNA, eye iris, etc. An individual's biometric information is recorded database. Various agencies like police, offices, bank lockers, etc. use biometrics software to detect the presence of

employees, customers, criminals, etc. even schools use biometrics these days to mark the entry or exit of students, teachers, and other staff members.

11. Many people watch content over different platforms on the Internet. Some examples of web entertainment platforms are YouTube, Facebook videos, IMDB, Netflix and more.

12. E-commerce websites monitor the customers likes, preferences and purchasing history to offer suggestions. They use programs called Reco Engines.

Answer in detail (150 words).

1. Data is divided into various types when recorded on a computer. Broadly, these types are sounds, text, numbers, videos and images. Data can be categorised, keeping in mind various factors. To begin with, we can divide data into:

   - Quantitative data
   - Qualitative data

   While the quantitative data is factual and can be measured or counted, qualitative data is descriptive and cannot be counted.

   Quantitative data is gathered by counting as opposed to qualitative data, which is gathered through observations.

   Quantitative data is numeric in nature, and therefore, is analysed through statistics. Qualitative data, on the other hand, is analysed through categories.

   Examples of quantitative data include marks, age, weight, number of patients, number of customers, etc. Colours of the flowers, contents of an email, hobbies, co-curricular activities are all examples of qualitative data.

   Quantitative data is further classified into:

   - Discrete
   - Continuous

   While both discrete and continuous data are quantitative data types, they are numeric in nature; they are different. Whereas discrete data is both measurable and countable, continuous data is only measurable. Discrete data has clear spaces. Continuous data can have any intervals. Let us understand with some examples.

Consider a situation when we order a certain number of dishes in a restaurant. The number of dishes we order is an example of discrete data, whereas the billed amount we pay is continuous data.

Data may be organised (structured) or unorganised (unstructured).

Unstructured data should be organised; only then it can be analysed.

2. Quantitative data is further classified into:
   - Discrete
   - Continuous

   While both discrete and continuous data are quantitative data types, they are numeric in nature; they are different. Whereas discrete data is both measurable and countable, continuous data is only measurable. Discrete data has clear spaces. Continuous data can have any intervals. Let us understand with some examples.

   Consider a situation when we order a certain number of dishes in a restaurant. The number of dishes that we order is an example of discrete data, whereas the billed amount we pay is continuous data.

3. Many people watch content over different platforms on the Internet. Some examples of entertainment platforms are YouTube, Facebook videos, IMDB, Netflix and many more. These platforms suggest a listing for you every time you log in. This is done with the help of data analysis. The backend programs, over a period of time, monitor which types of videos you play frequently. These programs get trained by this data and start predicting your choices and you get the suggestions. These use special programs called Reco Engines.

4. When data is collected, it is unstructured and just some information that is jumbled up and unclear. To use this information, this data needs to be organised and structured.

   Creating a database table is the next step that will make it easy to use. To organise data, it is placed into a table. This is called the database table. A database table contains only organised data. Data in a database table is organised in rows and columns.

   In this, each column represents a variable. A variable is an entity that contains some value. There are a certain number of observations. Once the data is organised it is easy for anyone to analyse it and use it further.

Example- If a collection of information containing names, marks in science and maths of students of a class needs to be presented in a database table.

Rima 72, 57

Saurabh 89, 64

Kriti 58, 70

Lara 32, 76

Kewal 67, 90

Mini 65, 69

Anima 58, 65

Name	Maths	Science
Rima	72	57
Saurabh	89	64
Kriti	58	70
Lara	32	76
Kewal	67	90
Mini	65	69
Anima	58	65

5. In your email some emails automatically go to the inbox while others end up in the spam folder. This is accomplished through data science. Spam filters (machine programs) are taught to recognise certain words in the mail, which classify them as spam. The program is trained using thousands of emails. After it gets trained, it segregates spam mails easily.

Chapter 2

Multiple choice questions.

1. b	2. a	3. b	4. a	5. d
6. b	7. c	8. a	9. b	10. d
11. b	12. d	13. all	14. a	15. d
16. b				

Answer the following questions in short (100 words).

1. Data Science is one of the technologies behind Artificial Intelligence. It structures, organises, and makes data interpretable. It is a field that involves a combined study of scientific methods, mathematics, statistics and coding to develop a system. Such a system extracts meaningful insights from data. New emerging technologies utilise data to bring out smart products. In simplest terms, the science of studying data is called data science.

2. Expert System is a computer system that emulates, or acts in all respects, with the decision-making capabilities of a human expert.

3. Data rules every sphere of life. Without data, there would be no technologies or systems. AI is completely based on data.

4. One of the primary industries to benefit from data sciences is retail and e-commerce. It is used not just for forecasting sales of goods and services but also for predicting trends. In addition, these intelligent systems identify a potential customer base while optimising price structures for a particular section of consumers.

5. Various job profiles related to data science are being developed to cater to the needs of the organisations. Companies like Google, Microsoft, Amazon and many more are expanding manifold in the field of applied data science. Three careers in this field are Data Scientists, Data Analysts and Data Architects.

6. Data Scientists look for problem areas, examine the current trends and predict the future ones. Knowledge of mathematics, statistics, and computer science help data scientists develop actionable plans for organisations after studying a huge amount of data, structured or unstructured (big data).

Data Analysts help to analyse the data and examine the trends. They work on specific problems and analyse structured data. Their knowledge in mathematics, statistics and computer science helps them create AI models.

7. Binary classification where the output of the classification is one of the two choices.
8. Predictive modelling helps to predict the outcome of a diagnosis given the previous data of the patients. It provides helpful insights to doctors and medical practitioners.
9. Data Science is also applied to the feedback provided by the customers. This is called sentiment analysis.
10. They analyse the data and examine the trends. They work on specific problems and analyse structured data. Their knowledge in mathematics, statistics and computer science helps them create AI models.
11. It is another technique of machine learning. It is a feedback-based system, meaning that the program learns to behave in an environment by performing the actions and getting feedback on the results of actions.
12. When new data is introduced to the model. This is called training data. Its accuracy gets better and better when exposed to more and more training data. In order to achieve this, appropriate techniques, such as supervised and unsupervised, are followed. The supervised technique is also known as the classification technique. This method classifies data with the help of class labels.
13. Clustering: Used for unsupervised learning. Dataset is not organised under labels.
14. Data science looks for patterns and relationships between the data and the required prediction. It tries to make predictions for new datasets which it has never seen before.
15. Regression is a method mainly used for making predictions based on some numerical values (stored in variables). The output of regression is also numeric. This forecasting method is mostly used for predicting weather conditions, making sales targets, looking at future marketing trends, etc.

Answer in detail (150 words).

1. The scope of applications of data sciences is broad and can be used in multiple categories.

Fraud Detection: More and more banks are making use of intelligent systems to track transactions made by credit cards holders. This helps them in detecting fraudulent activities, thereby labelling the customers or transactions as fraudulent or genuine. Banks use smart systems for insurance and accounting also. They analyse the investment patterns of customers and suggest offers and more investments. An unexpected change in data patterns can often be a sign of something going wrong or possible fraud.

Healthcare: There is a huge impact of data science on healthcare. The various industries in healthcare that use data science are:

- Genetics and Genomics
- Predictive Modelling for Diagnosis

Genetics and Genomics: Data Science helps find biological connections between genetics, risk of diseases, and drug response. An intelligent model applies statistical techniques to genomic sequences, allowing scientists to understand the complexities of genetic structures in detail. Genetic risk prediction is a giant leap towards more personalised healthcare. Predictive modelling helps to predict the outcome of a diagnosis given the previous data of the patients. Therefore, it provides helpful insights to doctors and medical practitioners.

Imagine a system predicting how well a person will respond to medicine by simply collecting and analysing data based on his past health.

Internet Searches: Data Science is evolving Internet searches. All the search engines, such as Google, Bing, AOL, etc., use data science algorithms to bring out results for the searched query. All this is done in a fraction of seconds!

GD: take only the pic part; no text

E-commerce: One of the primary industries to benefit from data sciences is retail and e-commerce. It is used not just for forecasting sales of goods and services but also for predicting trends. In addition, these intelligent systems identify a potential customer base while optimising price structures for a particular section of consumers.

2.

Classification	Clustering
Is used for supervised learning.	Is used for unsupervised learning.
Dataset is organised under labels.	Dataset is not organised under labels.
Training and testing data is used.	Training and testing data is not used.
Is more complex.	Is less complex.

3. Data Science has been most impactful in developing intelligent vehicles, such as self-driving cars. These are also known as driverless cars.

   Data Science has also helped make smart systems that monitor routes and share details with the drivers in real-time. For example, if a route is congested, the system suggests an alternate route. They also monitor fuel consumption patterns, vehicle routes, breakdowns, etc. Intelligent models continuously inspect driving environments for drivers. The goal is to provide safe environments.

   Data science has also impacted air transport. Various airlines use smart systems to predict flight arrivals and delays, project the most lucrative routes between two destinations and monitor customer behaviour regarding booking dates, seats, destinations, etc.

4. Techniques to analyse data widely depend on its type. The model looks for patterns and relationships between the existing data, called the testing data, and the required prediction in data science. New data is introduced to the model. This is called training data. Its accuracy gets better and better when exposed to more and more training data. In order to achieve this, appropriate techniques, such as supervised and unsupervised, are followed.

   The supervised technique is also known as the classification technique. This method classifies data with the help of class labels. An example of classification technique:

   A customer is considered as safe/ risky according to his Blood Pressure readings and Age in the health insurance application process. This is supervised learning, where the goal is to build a model which can classify new data.

   The unsupervised technique is also known as the clustering technique. Though it is similar to classification, it doesn't give data any labels. An example of clustering is a grouping of students in a class according to their age and height.

5. Reinforcement learning is another technique of machine learning. It is feedback-based, meaning that the program learns to behave in an environment by performing the actions and getting feedback on the results of actions. A good result generates positive feedback, whereas a bad result generates negative feedback. This can be considered as 'reward' or 'punishment'. As more and more data is fed, the model/machine is reinforced with positive behaviour. As a result, it learns to give correct outputs.

   If you want your dog to train your dog to sit, you would need to give him certain instructions. If the dog obeys, it gets a reward - a biscuit. If he doesn't obey, he wouldn't. The dog will learn this after some time. The reward in data science is feedback, an algorithm that is applied to many applications in daily life.

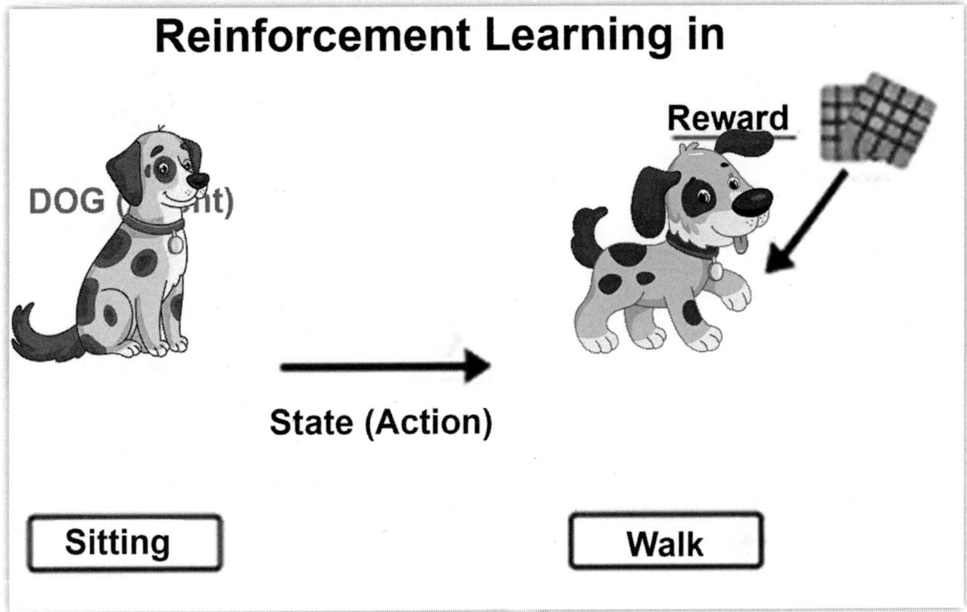

Chapter 3

Multiple choice questions.

1. c	2. b	3. a	4. a	5. d
6. b	7. c	8. a	9. b	10. a
11. d	12. a	13. c	14. a	15. c
16. a	17. d			

Answer the following questions in short (100 words).

1. There are five stages of the data life cycle. These are as follows-
   - Project definition
   - Data collection
   - Data visualisation
   - Data modelling
   - Evaluation and deployment
2. A Project Definition is outlining the project requirements. It is the first step and a crucial step without which data collection is not possible.
3. After the business problem is identified, data related to it is collected. This data is gathered from various sources called the data sources. Two sources of data collection are online and offline.
4. An analysis between two variables to determine their relationship is called Bivariate.
5. Quality of data influences the results. Therefore maintaining the quality of data is important. Two data factors that should be checked while collecting it are as follows-

   a. **Quality Check:** It is essential to check the quality of data before analysing it. As mentioned earlier, the bad quality of data may result in poor or misleading outcomes. Hence, it is essential to collect data that is relevant and acquired from reliable sources.

b. **Complete data collection:** Another factor to consider while collecting data is to check if the complete set of data is collected. Fractured data again may result in wrong analysis.

6. Organisations banks, schools, hospitals, travel agencies, have their records stored in databases. However, these are not available for everyone to access. Proper permissions should be taken while collecting data.

7. This step involves identifying the end-users of the analysis of data collected based on their expectations, how tech-savvy are they and they will be able to interpret the reports that are generated after data analysis. This helps in detailing and documentation of the outcomes expected.

8. A few data visualization tools are - MS Excel, MapR, Microsoft Power BI, Google Chart, Qlik Infogram and Tableau.

9. The three types of data analysis are as follows:

   - **Univariate:** analysis is the analysis of one variable.
   - **Bivariate:** Analysis is between two variables to determine their relationship
   - **Multivariate:** Analysis is of multiple outcome variables

10. Principal components analysis is done to convert correlated variables into a smaller number of uncorrelated variables.

11. A line chart is a data visualisation tool. It displays information as a series of data points called 'markers' connected by line segments. These are straight lines.

12. A Scatter plot displays data that doesn't have continuity. Any dot on the plot represents a value in the data set. Two data sets can also be represented in two colour dots.

13. Regression analysis predicts future possibilities based on the datasets collected earlier. It is also used to determine risk assessments.

    Cohort analysis compares data related to groups and cohorts.

14. If a hotel chain wants to predict how many customers will stay in a certain location in the winter vacations, they will use the historical data to find it. This will help them to plan accordingly.

15. Five types of charts and graphs are Bar graphs, column charts, line graphs, pie charts and bubble charts.

16. Histogram resembles a bar graph and represents the probable distribution of continuous numerical data. The parameters of the function include- variable and bin, which is the range of values. The bins are consecutive, non-overlapping intervals of a variable.

Answer in detail (150 words).

1 Data collection- the first stage of data cycle stage is when the data professionals collect the data. After the business problem is identified, data related to it is collected. This data is gathered from various sources called data sources. These sources are available either online or even offline.

Online data collection sources includes getting information from digital records of organisations, government portals, reliable websites like Kaggle and World organisations' statistical websites.

Many organisations, such as banks, schools, hospitals, travel agencies, etc., have their records stored in databases. However, these are not available for everyone to access. Therefore, proper permissions should be taken while collecting data, or data which is available for public usage should be collected.

2. Types of analysis based on variables include analysis of one variable, analysis between two variables to determine their relationship, analysis of multiple outcome variables and analysis to convert correlated variables into a smaller number of uncorrelated variables.

Displaying data through various types of charts, for example, bar charts, scatter and density plots, etc., analysts can study the variables and relationships between them.

Regression Analysis helps to find out the relationships between variables in the data. It helps to specify the independent (predictor variables) and dependent (response variables) nature of the variables.

3. Analysed data requires proper visualisation. The popular adage 'a picture tells a thousand words' holds true in the case of data analysis. Data visualisation means displaying data pictorially, either through graphs and charts. Data is visually represented to give clear information to the users. It is one of the steps in data analysis or data science. To convey ideas effectively, we must provide insights into complex data in a more interesting manner. Visualising any kind of data leads to better and easier understanding.

4. Analysed data requires proper visualisation. Once the data is collected and analysed, the next step involves selecting an appropriate visualisation tool. There are charts and graphs that can be selected. A line chart displays information as a series of data points called 'markers' connected by line segments. These are straight lines. A dot in a scatter plot represents each value in the data set. This type of plot displays data that doesn't have continuity. Two different data sets can be displayed as each having different coloured dots.

5. A bar chart is a visualisation tool that gives clarity to any data, It is a graph that displays data in rectangular bars, either vertically or horizontally.

   Example

   Data of rainfall for two years:

	1998	1999
June	20	25
July	36	34
August	32	31
September	18	16

Chapter 4

Multiple choice questions.

1. b	2. a	3. b	4. b	5. a
6. a	7. b	8. c	9. b	10. c
11. d	12. c	13. a	14. d	15. c

Answer the following questions in short (100 words).

1. AI means Artificial Intelligence, in which work is done by intelligent machines independently.

2. Text data is initial or raw data that is unorganised and unstructured. When high-quality information is sieved from a large volume of text, it is called text data analysis or text mining.

3. Smart virtual assistants like Amazon's Alexa, Apple's Siri and Microsoft's Cortana use voice recognition and inference techniques of NLP to provide useful responses. They not only detect our speech but also understand it and help us do our tasks.

4. Two examples of best online chatbots are as follows -

   a. **Endurance:** A Companion for Dementia Patients: Chats with patients who have Alzheimer's or Dementia.

   b. **MedWhat:** Makes faster medical diagnosis

5. Intelligent machines see and understand digital images and videos and then make predictions or decisions. The entire process involves these steps: real object image acquisition screening image analysing project information making a decision.

6. **There are three types of Artificial Intelligence:**

   a. Artificial Narrow Intelligence (ANI), which has a narrow range of abilities. It mainly focuses on one problem and one solution. Examples are Siri, Alexa and Cortana.

   b. Artificial General Intelligence (AGI), which is on par with human capabilities.

   c. Artificial Super Intelligence (ASI) is more capable than the human brain and surpasses human capabilities.

7. AI refers to the ability of machines to perform cognitive tasks like thinking, perceiving, learning, problem-solving and decision making. Initially conceived as a technology that could mimic human intelligence, AI has evolved in ways that far exceed its original conception.

8. AI, DL and ML may look similar but there is a basic difference between these terms.

   Machine Learning is a subset of Artificial Intelligence and deep learning is a subset of Machine Learning.

9. The prediction is the probability of outcomes that could arise when an algorithm is executed. For example, our email service provider learns to identify spam by looking at lots and lots of examples which we had earlier marked as spam. It predicts when shown a new email, whether it's spam or not.

10. "AI refers to the ability of machines to perform cognitive tasks like thinking, perceiving, learning, problem-solving and decision making. Initially conceived as a technology that could mimic human intelligence, AI has evolved in ways that far exceed its original conception. With incredible advances made in data collection, processing and computation power, intelligent systems can now be deployed to take over a variety of tasks, enable connectivity and enhance productivity."

11. One of the most common applications of Natural Language Processing is a chatbot. These are mainly used to provide customer service.

12. NLP (Natural Language Processing) is an area of AI concerned with the interactions between computer and human languages.

13. Deep Learning is a subset of Machine Learning where machines are taught to self-design and generate algorithms. Algorithms in Deep Learning are inspired by the structure of a human brain and use complex multi-layered neural networks.

Answer in detail (150 words).

1. There is a load of information available in today's world. Information overload has become a problem when a person needs specific information on something from a knowledge base. Automatic summarisation follows the 3C rule- crisp, concise and cohesive information imparting. It avoids redundancy from multiple resources. It not only provides crisp information but also understands the emotional meanings within the information. An example is collecting data from a social media site.

2. Data is gathered, cleaned, and analysed to give insights and make predictions We see things through our eyes. Intelligent machines 'see' things through digita images. Intelligent machines see and understand digital images and videos anc then make predictions or decisions. The entire process involves the following steps Real object, image aquisition, screening image, analysing, processing informatior and making decision.

3. There are three types of Artificial Intelligence:

   a. Artificial Narrow Intelligence (ANI), which has a narrow range of abilities. I mainly focuses on one problem and one solution. Examples are Siri, Alexa anc Cortana.

   b. Artificial General Intelligence (AGI), which is on par with human capabilities.

   c. Artificial Super Intelligence (ASI) is more capable than the human brain anc surpasses human capabilities.

4. Computers are everywhere today. It is inconceivable to carry out our daily lives while not employing a computer in some way or the other. We tend to use computers all the time unwittingly, like video games, cars, online banking, televisions, mobile phones and even toys. That is why computers must become more intelligent to make our lives better. since the invention of the computer, science fiction has made us believe in the likelihood of super-intelligent computers. Technology has developed at tremendous speed within the past few decades and has integrated AI in our lives Typical examples are: GPS Navigators, Universal remote controls, Amazon Alexa and Apple Siri. AI, is a field of computer science that tries to simulate characteristics of human intelligence or senses. These comprise learning, reasoning, and adapting.

   The computer programs written explicitly for this purpose perform tasks such as recognising and comprehending human speech, developing simulations, and analysing an immense amount of data to derive useful information.

5. Machine Learning is a subset of Artificial Intelligence and is concerned with designing and developing algorithms that allow computers to evolve behaviours based on experimental data. The idea behind machine learning is to make machines self-reliant in learning to provide accurate outcomes/ predictions or make correct decisions.